Following God's

Plan for Your Life

Fiat!

Following God's Plan for Your Life

A Spiritual Formation Program Presented by Fr. Zachary of the Mother of God, SOLT

Fiat! Following God's Plan for Your Life

A Spiritual Formation Program
Presented by Fr. Zachary of the Mother of God, SOLT

First edition, first printing in USA
ISBN: 978-193525730-1

Unless otherwise noted, all Scripture quotations (except those within citations)
have been taken from the Revised Standard Version of the Holy Bible Second Catholic
Edition. The Revised Standard Version of the Holy Bible, the Old Testament, ©1952;
the Apocrypha, ©1957; the New Testament, ©1946; Catholic Edition of the Old
Testament, incorporating the Apocrypha, ©1966; the Catholic Edition of the New
Testament, ©1965, by the Division of Christian Education of the National Council
of the Churches of Christ in the United States of America.

Excerpts from the English translation of the *Catechism of the Catholic Church* for
use in the United States of America, second edition copyright ©2000, United States
Conference of Catholic Bishops—Libreria Editrice Vaticana. Used with permission.

Excerpts from the English translation of the *Compendium of the Catechism
of the Catholic Church* for use in the United States of America copyright
©2006, United States Conference of Catholic Bishops—Libreria Editrice Vaticana.
Used with permission.

To order copies, please visit
www.OurLadyLovesYou.org

Book and cover design
Suzanne C. Hurtig, www.SuzanneHurtigDesign.com

JMJ + OBT

Fiat! is dedicated to the One, Holy, and Triune God:
Father, Son, and Holy Spirit.

Fiat! is also dedicated to Our Lady of the Most Holy Trinity,
St. Joseph, and all the Holy Angels and Saints.

Fiat! is to teach us to live for the honor and glory of God,
the exaltation of His Majesty,
and the manifestation of His greatness.

Dear Edward,
Become a Saint!
Our Lady Loves you!
Fiat! JTM SAT

Table of Contents

Invitation

JMJ + OBT

Omnia pro Iesu per Mariam!

JESUS IS THE ANSWER! All of the questions that come from the human heart can be answered in that Name above all other names, "Jesus." All of the longings, aspirations, needs, desires and hopes of mankind are fulfilled in God—Father, Son and Holy Spirit—in whose image we are created (cf. *CCC* 1, 27, 68). Jesus is the answer that God the Father speaks to the human heart, so that we may come to the peace, joy and love that God created us to enjoy. To those whose hearts are open and listening, the Holy Spirit speaks the Eternal Word of the Father: "Jesus."

Many people are asking for answers to the deepest questions of the human heart. Many people are asking, "What is the purpose and meaning of my life?" Many people are asking, "How do I pray so I can have a living relationship with God?" "How can I pray so that I can find the Plan of God in my life?" "How can I pray so that I can say YES to Jesus and fulfill the destiny God has for me and mankind?" Many people are asking, "What does it mean to be created in the image and likeness of God?" "How can I live a holy and virtuous life?" Many people are asking, "How do I please God just like Our Blessed Mother, Mary, and say FIAT to the Most Holy Trinity each moment of my life?"

In faithfully listening to the Eternal Word of the Father, Our Lady gave her "Fiat!" In freely giving her "Fiat!"—an absolute and unqualified "Yes!" to the Plan of God—Our Lady gave (and continually gives) her "Fiat!" to Jesus, Who is the Answer. **Our Blessed Mother, Mary, a human person, is the model of a heart open to Jesus.** In her Immaculate Heart, Our Lady perfectly loves God and ponders His Word so intimately that, as St. Augustine noted, "Mary conceived in her heart before she conceived in her womb." At the announcement of God's Word by the Angel Gabriel, she gave her "Fiat!" and by the power of the Holy Spirit, the Word became Flesh and dwelt among us.

Our Blessed Mother is one of us, the one who gave all of herself to Jesus, Who is the Answer. She shows us that it is possible (with the grace of God) to give ourselves completely and absolutely to Jesus. *"With the grace of God"* must be emphasized. Our Lady knows that while she is our great advocate and the mediatrix of all graces, she could neither assume nor fulfill her mission without the Holy Spirit, who is "the origin and source of our sanctification" as human persons (*CCC* 190; cf. 747). "Sanctification" refers fundamentally to the gift of "sanctifying grace," by which we are made holy and become children of God (*CCC* 1999, 2000), and it can also refer to our growth in holiness through a life of Christian virtue (*CCC* 2008, 2012-16).

Our Lady is rightly called "Full of Grace," and grace empowers her to always give her "Fiat!" to the Divine Plan of Love of the Most Holy

Trinity, announced in Jesus. This book is called *Fiat!* because we need to learn from Our Lady how to perfectly relate to the Most Holy Trinity, Who asks us to say "Fiat!" to the Divine Plan of Love. The Most Holy Trinity asks us to give our own personal "Fiat!" to Jesus. This means that we are to give all of our lives, completely and absolutely, to Jesus.

Fiat! is given because many people are asking important questions, but in order to receive the answers they need to go to Jesus and receive spiritual direction from Him, Who is the Answer. Just like Our Blessed Mother, *Fiat!* always points you to Jesus, Who is the Way, the Truth and the Life. This book is called *Fiat!* because it describes how to say "Yes!" to Jesus. *Fiat!* is given so that you may find the answers to the deepest longings of your heart. *Fiat!* is given so that you may become happy, holy and reach heaven. *Fiat!* is given so that you may imitate Mary, become like Jesus, and live for the Triune God. *Fiat!* is given so that you may find Jesus for yourself. We pray that when you are ready, you will hear the sweetest Word ever spoken to your open and listening heart. May you hear the answer to your every question as the voice of the Holy Spirit speaks the Eternal Word of the Father: "Jesus."

Through the intercession of Our Lady, St. Joseph, St. Michael, St. Peter, St. Paul, St. John, St. James, St. Thérèse, St. Rita, St. Louis Marie de Montfort, St. Philomena, St. Jude, St. Nicholas, St. Alphonsus, St. Peter Chrysologus, St. Zachary, St. Elizabeth, St. John the Baptist, St. Perpetua, St. Felicity, St. Francis, St. Veronica Guiliani, St. Joan of Arc, St. Louis, St. Joseph Calasanz, St. Charles Borromeo, St. Padre Pio, St. Patrick, St. Bridget, St. Columban and all the Holy Angels and Saints, may you be abundantly blessed in the Covenant of Communion of the

Most Holy Trinity—with my Priestly blessing, Father Zachary of the Mother of God, SOLT.

. . . .

Many people are asking ... "What is formation?"

Not just Information—"Formation"

You have come to a formation program. *This program is not just about information, it's about formation.* God Himself, your Father, is going to form you in Jesus Christ so that He can look upon you with love and smile upon you and bless you. For in Jesus, Our Father gives us every spiritual blessing.

Divine Way of Love

Our Father's desire is to see Jesus Christ come alive in our lives. Jesus reveals the meaning of life to us. He came from heaven to reveal the meaning of life to us. Jesus Christ reveals man to himself. We are mysteries to ourselves, so Jesus came to unfold that mystery, to let us know that we are loved, and to empower us so that we can return this love. Alone, we are only capable of a human way of love, but we are invited to a Divine way of love.

Would you like to receive this Divine Way of Love? Would you like to be formed into this Divine Way of Love? Our heavenly Father is forming us in Jesus Christ every moment of our lives. What a blessed life that we are all invited to embrace—if we can only accept it.

Assuredly, this gift is so precious that many people hesitate at the call to greatness—but you are created for greatness in God's Love. No matter what has happened in your life, know that God loves you and that He has a plan for your life. He will form you in His beloved Son, Jesus Christ. You can participate in the life of God. We all need help, though, and we all have to begin somewhere. Today if you hear His voice—harden not your hearts. Respond to this invitation.

We are all invited (by God Himself) to know that He has a plan for each of our lives, to respond to this plan, and to come to this plan like Our Blessed Mother. Our Blessed Mother Mary, a human person (one of us) responds perfectly with every beat of her heart and with every breath. In every moment of her life she said "yes" to God's plan, so we give her special veneration or reverential honor. Only God is to be worshiped. Yet clearly, Our Blessed Mother deserves to be honored above all human persons because of her unparalleled response to God.

As our mother, Mary desires to train us and help us to be formed. Training ... formation ... they are very similar and they go together. Mary wants to form us in Christ as well, because as a mother, she loves to bring forth life. Jesus came from heaven to give us life: abundant life, eternal life. Today we ask the Holy Spirit to open our hearts to receive this life. No matter what has happened in your life, today is a new day. We are a redeemed people. Jesus Christ is our Savior—He redeemed us. Just as the sun rises everyday to remind us of new life (the fresh start that He won for us), make the decision to let Our Blessed Mother lead you to her Son, Jesus Christ. Let Our Father draw you to His beloved Son. Let the Holy Spirit guide you. Let Him form you. Let Him breathe upon you and embrace you. God loves you!

As we journey through this formation program, we will continue to develop what formation entails. In the events and circumstances of your daily lives, God will be forming you in wisdom, age and grace to come to the full measure of the mature Christ. You will begin to understand how God is working in your life. We will teach you how to relate with God so that you can see His loving hand in everything that has happened in your life. We will teach you how Our Blessed Mother cares for you with a tender affection and a loving concern (as only a mother can) to form you in Jesus.

Everything in your life has purpose and meaning. Everything. We need to put on the mind of Christ in order to respond generously, just as Christ responds to the will of the Father.

Spiritual formation is a lifelong adventure. This book can serve as the beginning of the greatest adventure of your life. It can also be your companion as you move toward your destiny.

Moreover, in the Society of Our Lady of the Most Holy Trinity, we have a three-year program of formation as a foundation for your life. You can learn how God worked in the life of the Blessed Virgin Mary, Our Lady of the Most Holy Trinity—a human person like us. You will learn how Our Lady said "yes" to God's plan every moment of her life. You will follow her life and parallel it to your own.

Too many people separate themselves from Our Blessed Mother because of her holiness. Her holiness should draw us in. Jesus gave her to us at the foot of the Cross—His last gift before He commended His Spirit into the hands of the Father. This gift of Our Lady is a tremendous gift. We learn from her life how God cares for our life. In this program, we follow her life to better understand how God formed her. Recognizing God's hand in the life of Our Blessed Mother and in our own is what formation is all about. Then, in the circumstances of our daily life, we will experience this formation. This formation is personal. It's also communal.

Following each teaching, you will have the opportunity to integrate the lessons into your life. Remember, it's not just about formation, it's about the relationship that blossoms from this formation. It's a living and active reality. It's your destiny. And so we begin...

Happiness & Holiness

Every thinking person asks the three most important questions: "Why am I here?" "Where am I from?" "Where am I going?" The answer to all three questions is God—the most Holy Trinity—Father, Son and Holy Spirit.

The purpose and meaning of life is God. In His infinite love and goodness, God created all of us out of nothing. He gave us our life, and what a great gift it is. Moreover, God has a plan for our life. You see it in all of creation. God has a plan for everything. You see His goodness, His fingerprints in everything. When we order our lives to God we find our happiness, for God wants us to be happy. Do you know that? God wants us to be happy. We must understand that true happiness is the fruit of holiness. As noted in the Introduction, the Holy Spirit is "the origin and source of our sanctification" or holiness (*CCC* 190; cf. 747, 1989, 1995). We are made holy by receiving sanctifying grace at our baptism (*CCC* 1266) and we grow in holiness through a life of Christian virtue (*CCC* 2008, 2012-16). Thus, on a practical level, holiness is basically doing God's will and loving God for Himself above all things. And knowing God and doing His will makes us happy. So true happiness is the fruit of holiness.

Lasting happiness is not found in sensual pleasures like drinking, making money, or buying clothes. After pursuing worldly pleasures, laced with vanity, greed or gluttony, we find ourselves empty and alone. The world lures us with a false hope of happiness, then leaves us with a deep void.

On the other hand, when you know that you are loved by Almighty God, that He's got a purpose and a plan for your life, and that you have a destiny, you can truly live a happy life—one that is filled with purpose and meaning—one that is filled with God's peace and joy.

Today, God has called you (in His love) to free you from the fears and the worries and the confusion that this world causes. God desires to liberate you from these worldly chains by giving you the truth that you are willed and loved. Do you know that? You are willed and loved. Before all of creation, in His mind's eye, in His infinite goodness, in His infinite wisdom and love—God knew you. Our Father chose to create *you*. He made you special and He loves you. You were created in His love, so you are precious. You were willed by God to exist and to know Him, love Him and serve Him, and to be happy with Him forever. That's what the *Baltimore Catechism* teaches. We have these basic questions addressed in the *Baltimore Catechism*: Who created everything? God. Who created me? God. Why did He create me? To know, love and serve Him and be happy with Him forever.

In biblical terms, we must recognize that to know God means to be intimate with Him. We love the Word—the living Word of God, Jesus Christ. Our lives are present in this Word. *All* of our lives are united in the Word, which means that all of our lives are mystically connected right here in the Word of God. Our lives are spelled out in this Word. We won't understand the fullness of the Word until everyone's life has been lived (cf. *CCC* 1039). That's why we pray that everyone will have a chance to be born and live a full life. Life is sacred from conception to natural death. We need to protect life because each life is a unique, precious and unrepeatable manifestation of God's love—just like you are.

As we live our lives in the Word, empowered by the sacraments in the Catholic Church, there is more understanding of God's love— more understanding of who God is. We are all unique, precious and unrepeatable manifestations of God. So we need each other to live our lives in Jesus Christ.

Don't be deceived by the enemy, the devil. Don't be deceived by the world. Don't be drawn away from God through the desires of the flesh. You have a purpose and a plan to fulfill in God's love. God wants you to know Him. That's why Jesus came from heaven: to reveal God's love and God's plan in the Word. God's Word is transmitted to us in Sacred Scripture and Sacred Tradition, which collectively contain the "Deposit of Faith" that the Magisterium faithfully expounds in providing us with the Church's teachings on faith and morals. The Magisterium is the Church's teaching office and is comprised of the Pope and the bishops in communion with him.

Overview of Formation Program

We will describe how God reveals His plan for our lives. For now, simply understand that God willed that you exist, and that He thus loves you. We are not accidents. We were created because God loves us. God created us in His image and likeness so that we can dwell in communion with Him.

Prayer will help you to know God, love God, serve God and be happy with Him forever. Prayer will help you find this plan of God in every moment of your life. You will move from understanding that God has a purpose and a plan for your life (the purpose and meaning of life) into prayer.

Then we will demonstrate why we were created in God's image and likeness and how it brings us to communion with Him. Then we will move into the universal call to holiness and virtue. A virtuous life is a beautiful life.

We will then explain how liturgy is Life. We will teach you about the Holy Sacrifice of the Mass, the Word, Sacred Tradition, and the Magisterium of the Church. We will explain the Eucharist—the gift of Jesus' Body, Blood, Soul and Divinity—really, truly and substantially present. Our Lord is given to us to strengthen us for our destiny—to fulfill His purpose and plan.

Consecration & "Fiat!"

We will lead you to a consecration to Jesus Christ (Wisdom Incarnate) through the hands of Our Blessed Mother. We will show you how Our Lady understood that she was created in God's love; that she was willed and loved; and that she was fulfilling a purpose and a plan in her life. God's plan for her was to be the Mother of Christ, who is God, so she is the Mother of God. Remember, God is God alone. Our Blessed Mother is a human person—a human person who understood that God had a purpose and a plan for her life and so she said, "Yes!

Be it done unto me according to Thy Word." These same words should flow from our heart every moment of our lives: "Fiat. Yes, God."

Jesus tells us to let our "yes" be "yes" and our "no" be "no." Let us say "yes" to God and "no" to the enemy. We say "no" to the world and "no" to the flesh. When you *always* give your "yes" to God, you will be happy and holy, and God willing, you will reach heaven—which is eternal happiness. This is your destiny—eternal happiness with God in heaven.

The Word of God is Living & Effective

The word of God is living and active, sharper than any two-edged sword... (Hebrews 4:12). It comes right into our lives and reveals to us the meaning of life. Our Holy Father, Pope Benedict XVI, speaking about the Word says, "It is the Word of God Himself who declares, 'Everyone who listens to these words of mine and acts on them will be like a wise man.' We are to let the Word of God penetrate our lives and in this way to know the fundamental truth of who we are, where we come from, where we must go and what path we must take in life."

Do you want to know who you are as God sees you? Do you want to know where you come from? Do you want to know where you must go—what path you must take in life? Our Blessed Mother will help you understand the Word of God because she said "yes" to the Word of God. Our Lady already had the Word of God in her heart before she conceived in her womb. She was properly disposed to say "yes" to God's plan as announced by the angel Gabriel at the Annunciation; you read this in the Word of God. The angel Gabriel was sent from heaven announcing the plan of God and Our Lady said, "Fiat." Therefore, *The Word became flesh and dwelt among us.*

Many people are asking ... "What is STMD?"

The answer to every question conceived in the human heart is "Jesus." Many people want to know, love and serve God so that they can be happy with Him forever in heaven. In order to have a solid foundation upon which to build your relationship with God, you must first have a solid formation. The foundation of this formation program is called "STMD" for short. The letters "STMD" stand for:

- Sacred Scripture

- Sacred Tradition

- Magisterium's faithful exposition of the Deposit of Faith, *i.e.,* providing the Church's official teaching drawn from Scripture and Tradition

Understanding each foundational element of your spiritual formation is essential. A short explanation of each one follows, so that you may *Always be prepared to make a defense to any one who calls you to account for the hope that is in you, yet do it with gentleness and reverence; and keep your conscience clear, so that, when you are abused, those who revile your good behavior in Christ may be put to shame. For it is better to suffer for doing right, if that should be God's will, than for doing wrong (1 Peter 3:15-17).*

Sacred Scripture

But as for you, continue in what you have learned and have

firmly believed, knowing from whom you learned it and how from
childhood you have been acquainted with the sacred writings
which are able to instruct you for salvation through faith in Christ
Jesus. All scripture is inspired by God and profitable for teaching,
for reproof, for correction, and for training in righteousness, that
the man of God may be complete, equipped for every good work
(II Timothy 3:14-17).

So here we have a perfect explanation of Sacred Scripture, straight
from Sacred Scripture! Through the power of the Holy Spirit, God
inspired many authors to write His Words, and they are collected in
the Canon of Sacred Scripture, which is more commonly called the
"Bible." The *Catechism of the Catholic Church* tells us in paragraph
81: "'*Sacred Scripture* is the speech of God as it is put down in writing
under the breath of the Holy Spirit.' (*Dei Verbum* 9)" When we read
the Bible, we are confident that we are reading the inspired Word of
God. Of course, we also know that St. John (the beloved disciple) has
testified that, *"There are also many other things that Jesus did, but*
if these were to be described individually, I do not think the whole
world would contain the books that would be written" (John 21:25).
This brings us quite naturally to Sacred Tradition.

Sacred Tradition

In testifying that "the whole world would not contain the books
that would be written" about all Jesus said and did, John gives us a
simple definition of "Sacred Tradition." The *Catechism of the Catholic*
Church further illuminates this point when it states that:

76 In keeping with the Lord's command, the Gospel was

handed on in two ways:

– *orally* "by the apostles who handed it on, by the spoken
word of their preaching, by the example they gave, by the
institutions they established, what they themselves had
received—whether from the lips of Christ, from his way
of life and his works, or whether they had learned it at the
prompting of the Holy Spirit"; (*Dei Verbum* 7)

– *in writing* "by those apostles and other men associated
with the apostles who, under the inspiration of the same
Holy Spirit, committed the message of salvation
to writing." (*Dei Verbum* 7)

We also hear the Great Commission of Jesus in Sacred Scripture, in
the Gospel of Matthew (28:18-20):

And Jesus came and said to them, "All authority in
heaven and on earth has been given to me. Go therefore
and make disciples of all nations, baptizing them in the
name of the Father and of the Son and of the Holy Spirit,
teaching them to observe all that I have commanded
you; and behold, I am with you always, to the close of
the age."

It is most beautiful that Our Lord and Savior gave the Apostles
authority to hand everything on *orally*. So the Apostles went forth
and preached the Good News (the Apostolic Tradition) without
even one book of the New Testament. You see, Jesus didn't give the
Apostles a written New Testament. He gave them a Commission,

with the authority to orally hand on all that He did and taught. The 27 written books of the New Testament are the fruit of the living Apostolic Tradition.

We learn more about the relationship of Sacred Scripture and Sacred Tradition when we read in the *Catechism* that:

81 "[Holy] *Tradition* transmits in its entirety the Word of God which has been entrusted to the apostles by Christ the Lord and the Holy Spirit. It transmits it to the successors of the apostles so that, enlightened by the Spirit of truth, they may faithfully preserve, expound and spread it abroad by their preaching." (*Dei Verbum* 9)

82 As a result the Church, to whom the transmission and interpretation of Revelation is entrusted, "does not derive her certainty about all revealed truths from the holy Scriptures alone. Both Scripture and Tradition must be accepted and honored with equal sentiments of devotion and reverence." (*Dei Verbum* 9)

Apostolic Tradition and Ecclesial Traditions

83 The Tradition here in question comes from the apostles and hands on what they received from Jesus' teaching and example and what they learned from the Holy Spirit. The first generation of Christians did not yet have a written New Testament, and the New Testament itself demonstrates the process of living Tradition.

Tradition is to be distinguished from the various

theological, disciplinary, liturgical or devotional traditions, born in the local churches over time. These are particular forms, adapted to different places and times, in which the great Tradition is expressed. In the light of Tradition, these cultural traditions can be retained, modified or even abandoned under the guidance of the Church's magisterium.

84 The apostles entrusted the "Sacred deposit" of the faith (the *depositum fidei*), (*Dei Verbum* 10§1; cf. 1 Tim 6:20; 2 Tim 1:12-14 [Vulg.]) contained in Sacred Scripture and Tradition, to the whole of the Church. "By adhering to [this heritage] the entire holy people, united to its pastors, remains always faithful to the teaching of the apostles, to the brotherhood, to the breaking of bread and the prayers. So, in maintaining, practicing, and professing the faith that has been handed on, there should be a remarkable harmony between the bishops and the faithful." (*Dei Verbum* 10§1; cf. Acts 2:42 (Gk.); Pius XII, apostolic constitution, *Munificentissimus Deus*, November 1, 1950: AAS 42 (1950), 756, taken along with the words of St. Cyprian, *EPIST.* 66, 8: CSEL 3, 2, 733: "The Church is the people united to its Priests, the flock adhering to its Shepherd."

The *Compendium of the Catechism of the Catholic Church* clearly answers the following questions regarding Sacred Tradition:

12. What is Apostolic Tradition?

Apostolic Tradition is the transmission of the message of Christ, brought about from the very beginnings of Christianity by means of preaching, bearing witness, institutions, worship, and inspired writings. The apostles transmitted all they received from Christ and learned from the Holy Spirit to their successors, the bishops, and through them to all generations until the end of the world.

13. In what ways does Apostolic Tradition occur?
Apostolic Tradition occurs in two ways: through the living transmission of the word of God (also simply called Tradition) and through Sacred Scripture which is the same proclamation of salvation in written form.

14. What is the relationship between Tradition and Sacred Scripture?
Tradition and Sacred Scripture are bound closely together and communicate one with the other. Each of them makes present and fruitful in the Church the mystery of Christ. They flow out of the same divine well-spring and together make up one sacred deposit of faith from which the Church derives her certainty about revelation.

15. To whom is the deposit of faith entrusted?
The Apostles entrusted the deposit of faith to the whole of the Church. Thanks to its supernatural sense of faith the people of God as a whole, assisted by the Holy Spirit and guided by the Magisterium of the Church, never ceases to welcome, to penetrate more deeply and to live more fully

from the gift of divine revelation.

16. To whom is given the task of authentically interpreting the deposit of faith?

The task of giving an authentic interpretation of the deposit of faith has been entrusted to the living teaching office of the Church alone, that is, to the successor of Peter, the Bishop of Rome, and to the bishops in communion with him. To this Magisterium, which in the service of the Word of God enjoys the certain charism of truth, belongs also the task of defining dogmas which are formulations of the truths contained in divine Revelation. The authority of the Magisterium also extends to those truths necessarily connected with Revelation.

The Magisterium of the Church

The foundation of the Magisterium is rooted in this beautiful exchange between Our Lord Jesus Christ and Saint Peter:

> *He said to them, "But who do you say that I am?" Simon Peter replied, "You are the Christ, the Son of the living God." And Jesus answered him, "Blessed are you, Simon Bar-Jona! For flesh and blood has not revealed this to you, but my Father who is in heaven. And I tell you, you are Peter, and on this rock I will build my church, and the powers of death shall not prevail against it. I will give you the keys of the kingdom of heaven, and whatever you bind on earth shall be bound in heaven,*

and whatever you loose on earth shall be loosed in heaven" (Matthew 16:15-19).

It is from the authority given by Jesus to Peter (who was, of course, the very first Pope) that the authority of the Magisterium is derived. The *Catechism of the Catholic Church* explains it this way:

85 "The task of giving an authentic interpretation of the Word of God, whether in its written form or in the form of Tradition, has been entrusted to the living teaching office of the Church alone. Its authority in this matter is exercised in the name of Jesus Christ." (*Dei Verbum* 10§2) This means that the task of interpretation has been entrusted to the bishops in communion with the successor of Peter, the Bishop of Rome.

86 "Yet this Magisterium is not superior to the Word of God, but is its servant. It teaches only what has been handed on to it. At the divine command and with the help of the Holy Spirit, it listens to this devotedly, guards it with dedication and expounds it faithfully. All that it proposes for belief as being divinely revealed is drawn from this single deposit of faith." (*Dei Verbum* 10§2)

87 Mindful of Christ's words to his apostles: "He who hears you, hears me," (Lk 10:16; cf. *Lumen Gentium* 20) the faithful receive with docility the teachings and directives that their pastors give them in different forms.

Finally, the *Compendium of the Catechism of the Catholic*

Church, in question number 17, explains to us the vital link between Scripture, Tradition and the Magisterium of the Church:

> Scripture, Tradition and the Magisterium are so closely united with each other that one of them cannot stand without the others. Working together, each in its own way, under the action of the one Holy Spirit, they all contribute effectively to the salvation of souls.

"Going Deeper": Applying STMD in Your Fiat! Formation

To help you better learn and apply the lessons of STMD, we'll be "going deep" with a special subsection at the end of each chapter, except Chapter Five. We'll reflect on relevant passages from Scripture, the writings of the saints and excerpts from the *Catechism of the Catholic Church*. As noted earlier, the "S" is for Scripture and the "T" is for Sacred Tradition. The orthodox writings of the saints are not Sacred Tradition *per se*, but they do provide, like the sayings of the early Church Fathers, a faithful "witness to the life-giving presence of this Tradition" in the Church (cf. *CCC* 78). The saints have embraced the richness of Sacred Tradition, and they are wonderful role models in living this divine gift. Thus, their intercession and their faithful writings should be our constant companions on our path of holiness.

Finally, as noted earlier, "MD" in STMD is the "the Magisterium's faithful exposition of the Deposit of Faith," in this case through the teachings of the Catechism. And similar to a good M.D., the Magisterium serves as a good "spiritual doctor," bringing us to good health in *the truth [that] will make [us] free... (John 8:32)*, and pointing us to effective "spiritual medicine" when needed, such as the sacraments and other means. Throughout salvation history, God has always established human leaders to guide his people, such as Abraham and Moses, and He does also in the New Covenant Church with the Magisterium, beginning with Peter and the other apostles, and then thereafter with the successors of Peter and the bishops (successors to the apostles) in communion with them. Thus, while the Bible is certainly God's sacred Word, we need a God-ordained Magisterium to ensure that Scripture's truths are properly discerned and safeguarded. Similarly, when questions arise within the Church about what is genuinely Catholic, we can always rely on the Magisterium to provide the truth. As Jesus promised Peter and the other Apostles, the powers of death shall not prevail against His Church (cf. Matthew 16:18).

This is why it's crucial for us to be properly rooted "STMD Catholics," Catholics who recognize Scripture, Tradition and the Deposit of Faith, but precisely as is faithfully safeguarded and expounded by the successor of Peter, the Pope and the bishops in communion with him. That is, by the authentic Magisterium. So with this deeper understanding of the foundational elements of this formation program, let's get started. May God richly bless you, and may Our Lady wrap her mantle around you as you enter into the journey toward holiness.

"How do I begin?"

Our Lady of the Most Holy Trinity welcomes you to the garden of her heart. And this spiritual formation program begins here, in Our Mother's Heart. No terrestrial garden compares with the goodness, truth, and beauty that the Triune God has placed in the Heart of Our Blessed Mother. SOLT receives the wonderful gift of Trinitarian-Marian Spirituality from Our Father through the tender heart of Our Blessed Mother. As you stroll through the Garden, allow her to show you all that she wishes to give you, her beloved child. Our Mother gives all of herself to us, and she forms and teaches us with the tender affection that only a mother can show. Enjoy your stroll through the Garden. May you emerge refreshed, with a renewed zeal for sharing her Heart with everyone.

On this journey of formation, there are many possible ways to proceed. We have itemized a few schedule options, and we encourage you to customize the program to best suit your personal and family needs. To optimize your formation, we invite you to visit our website at **www.OurLadyLovesYou.org** where an enhanced version of the program is available.

You should plan to spend *at least* one week with each chapter (formation topic). The truths contained in these teachings are so rich that you will need ample time to reflect upon them, to pray about them, and to put them into practice in your daily life.

Whatever pace you choose to travel, enjoy your time in the Garden of Our Lady's Heart.

A Note About Music

If you enjoy simple, unadorned vocal music, you may visit our website at **www.OurLadyLovesYou.org** to select a song that compliments the chapter you are studying. These songs were composed for our children's formation program, and offer a cheerful reminder of the main points covered in each teaching. You can locate suggested songs for each teaching at the end of each chapter under the heading "Mary's Children Sing!"

Suggestions for Pacing

Following are a few suggestions on pacing this formation program. Feel free to amend these options in any way you find helpful. Remember, for additional materials, you may access our website at **www.OurLadyLovesYou.org**. The following schedules will allow you to complete Chapters one through ten of this program on a 3-, 5- or 7-day per week cycle, over a period of 10 weeks. (Chapter 11 is to be approached in the manner specified in *Total Consecration to Jesus through Mary according to St. Louis Marie de Montfort.*)

3-Day per Week Schedule

- Day One—Read Chapter Topic and Day One Reflections

- Day Two—Day Two Reflections

- Day Three—Going Deeper with STMD

5-Day per Week Schedule

- Day One—Read Chapter Topic

- Day Two—Day One Reflections

- Day Three—Day Two Reflections

- Day Four—Going Deeper with STMD

- Day Five—Choose one topic from STMD to go even deeper

7-Day per Week Schedule

- Day One—Read Chapter Topic

- Day Two—Day One Reflection

- Day Three—Day Two Reflection

- Day Four—Sacred Scripture section of Going Deeper with STMD

- Day Five—Sacred Tradition section of Going Deeper with STMD

- Day Six—Magisterium section of Going Deeper with STMD

- Day Seven—Holy Hour with Jesus to reflect upon the teachings and seal the graces for the week

After trying one of these suggestions, if you need more time on a topic, PLEASE TAKE IT! Let the Holy Spirit guide you through this formation program. After all, God is the formator. If you choose to supplement this book with the materials on the website, consider following the schedule of our parish program, and review each topic for one full month according to the following schedule:

Week One—Priest Teaching on Topic

Week Two—Topic Facilitation #1

        (To help you to "dig deeper" into each topic)

Week Three—Topic Facilitation #2

        (To help you to "dig deeper" into each topic)

Week Four—Guided Holy Hour

        (To reflect and seal the graces for each teaching)

Please realize that whatever schedule you choose, God will bless your efforts. May you continue to be immersed in His love and mercy as you prepare to give your very own "Fiat!" to the Father as you learn to *Imitate Mary, Become Like Jesus and Live for the Triune God!*

Chapter One

"What is the purpose and meaning of my life?"

People are asking, "What is the purpose and meaning of my life?" The answer is: "Jesus." Everyone, every thinking person has three questions that they ask. "Why am I here?" "Where am I from?" "Where am I going?" The answer to all three questions is "God: the Most Holy Trinity, Father, Son and Holy Spirit."

Today's teaching is about the purpose and meaning of your life. The purpose and meaning of your life is God. You see, God, in His infinite love and goodness created you out of nothing. God has a plan, and we see it in all of creation. You see His goodness, His fingerprints in everything. When you turn your face to God, who is Love, and you order your life toward Him (the greatest of all Lovers) then you will find happiness.

Let's turn to Him now by praying the Lord's Prayer, known as the "Our Father." Let us pray this "perfect prayer" along with Jesus, the Eternal High Priest:

In the name of the Father and of the Son and of the Holy Spirit. Amen.

*Our Father who art in heaven, hallowed be Thy Name. Thy
Kingdom come. Thy will be done, on earth as it is in heaven.
Give us this day our daily bread, and forgive us our trespasses,
as we forgive those who trespass against us, and lead us not into
temptation, but deliver us from evil. Amen.*

Our Lady of the Most Holy Trinity, pray for us.

*In the name of the Father and of the Son and of the Holy
Spirit. Amen.*

Today, God has called you in His love to break you free from the
fears, worries, anxieties, and confusion that are caused by this world.
God desires to break you free so that you know that you are willed
and loved. Do you know that? You are willed and loved. Before all of
creation, in His mind's eye, in His infinite goodness, in His infinite
wisdom and love, Our Father chose to create you. You are precious
and He loves you. You were created in His love. You were willed by
God to exist—to know, love and serve Him, and be happy with Him
forever in heaven.

God wants us to be happy. Do you know that? God wants you to
be happy. We must recognize again that true happiness is the fruit of
holiness. As noted in the Introduction, on a practical level holiness is
basically doing God's will and loving Him above all things. Knowing
God and doing His will makes us happy.

True happiness does not consist in drinking, using drugs, buying
things, having a successful career, or experiencing any other worldly
pleasure. These physical stimulations give only temporary satisfaction
and result in worry, regret, and loneliness. These worldly sense
pleasures begin with a promise of fulfillment, but leave us empty and

alone. But, when you know that God has a Purpose and a Plan for your life—when you know that you are willed by God to exist and that you are precious to Him—then you can be truly happy.

Your life is unique and unrepeatable. We won't understand the fullness of the Word until everyone's life has been lived (cf. *CCC* 1039). That's why we pray that everyone has a chance to be born and have a full life. That's why life is sacred from conception to natural death. As we live out our lives in the Word, empowered by the sacraments in the Catholic Church, there is more understanding of God's love. There is more understanding of who God is. We are all unique, precious and unrepeatable manifestations of God. *All* brothers and sisters of the human family, young and old, rich and poor, preborn and born need to be in solidarity in Jesus Christ. When we live the unique, precious and unrepeatable life that God has planned for us we will be happy and we will please God, thereby bringing His blessings upon the whole human family.

Don't be deceived by the enemy, the devil. Don't be deceived by the world. Don't be drawn away from God by your sensual appetites. You have a purpose and a plan to fulfill in God's love. God wants you to know Him. That's why Jesus came from heaven: to reveal God's love and God's plan right here in the Word—right here in the teachings of the Catholic Church—in Sacred Tradition and Sacred Scripture and the Magisterium of the Catholic Church.

For now, understand that Almighty God, who holds the entire universe in His hands, willed that you exist. He loves you. Today is the day to embrace the purpose and meaning of your life in Jesus Christ. Today is the day to start living the plan of your life according to the will of God. Today is the day to accept the loving embrace of Jesus and be transformed in His love. "What is the purpose and meaning of my life?" "Jesus."

DAY ONE –

Reflecting with Mary on the Purpose and Meaning of Life

The "Our Father" prayer will be unfolded in the first year of formation. The Church teaches us that there is One God in three Divine Persons: Father, Son and Holy Spirit. Just like Our Blessed Mother Mary, we should relate to each of these Divine Persons as Individuals and as a communion of Divine Persons. We need to have a relationship with each Person of the Trinity. And we should love God first and foremost for who He is, not what He can do for us, although we can certainly be confident of His love and mercy, given Jesus' redemptive sacrifice on our behalf. For now, we want to focus on the first two words of this prayer, "Our Father." Think about the gift of having the perfect Father in heaven. Ask Our Blessed Mother to gift you with her relationship as the perfect child of the Father, as you pray this familiar prayer.

In the name of the Father and of the Son and of the Holy Spirit. Amen.

Our Father who art in heaven, hallowed be Thy Name. Thy Kingdom come. Thy will be done, on earth as it is in heaven. Give us this day our daily bread, and forgive us our trespasses, as we forgive those who trespass against us, and lead us not into temptation, but deliver us from evil. Amen.

Our Lady of the Most Holy Trinity, pray for us.

In the name of the Father and of the Son and of the Holy Spirit. Amen.

Before all of creation, in His mind's eye, in His infinite goodness, in His infinite wisdom and love, Our Father chose to create you. He loves you. You were created in His love. You were willed by God to exist and "to know Him, love Him and serve Him, and be happy with Him forever." God loves you so much!

Take a moment now to thank your perfect Father for creating you and giving you a purpose and meaning. Write a short "Thank You Note" to your Father.

Dear Heavenly Father,

THANK YOU for _____

_____

_____

_____

Your Grateful Child,

_____

Our Blessed Mother knew that she was a beloved daughter in the eyes of the Father. She knew that she was a true child of God Most High. As God's purpose and meaning for her life unfolded, she also understood herself as Mother and Disciple of the Son, and Spouse and Sanctuary of the Holy Spirit. She understood herself in the light of these blessed relationships, and lived a life worthy of the name "Christian." If we also desire to be worthy of the Name, we need to imitate Our Lady so that she can lead us to become like Jesus and live for the Triune God.

Take some time to quietly contemplate the following truths that the Most Blessed Trinity wants you to claim for your own.

You may want to preface each statement with, "I claim the Truth that… "

- The Most Holy Trinity wants me to think of myself as a true child of God Most High.

- The Most Holy Trinity wants me to understand myself as a disciple of the Son.

- The Most Holy Trinity wants me to embrace the incredible gift of being a temple of the Holy Spirit.

DAY TWO – The Truth About Your Life

The truth that God preordained your life from all eternity will truly set you free. You need to realize that the enemy does not want you to know this fact. He knows the power of truth. This truth must deeply penetrate our hearts so that we can be both happy and holy, just like Our Lady. Remember, true happiness is the fruit of holiness! Our Lady absolutely knew this, for she was also in the mind of the Father from all eternity. She understood herself as a beloved Daughter of the Father. This knowledge was essential for her to fulfill the purpose and meaning that God ordained for her life.

Ask yourself:

- How does it change the way I think of myself to know that I have been in the mind of God for all eternity?

- Am I beginning to get a glimpse of the purpose and meaning God has given to my life?

The truth is: I am a "unique, precious and unrepeatable manifestation of God's love." How does this truth change the way I view myself and others?

As you reflect on the meditations throughout this book, you will have many little epiphanies, or what some call "Aha!" moments. When the Holy Spirit touches your heart with His revealed truth, you need to claim that truth for yourself. It is important to claim truth and grace as soon as we recognize them, and ask the Holy Spirit to seal these truths and graces in our souls (from Mass, Reconciliation, Scripture, Formation, Retreats, etc). It is a very simple but powerful way to engage your heart.

You simply pray:

Blessed Mother and Guardian Angel, please gather all the graces from these truths; and please, Holy Spirit, seal them in my soul forever so that they may bear fruit in time and in eternity. Amen.

The present moment is always the best time to seal truths and graces, so let's do it right now.

Let us pray:

Dear Father, Son and Holy Spirit, thank you for all you have revealed to me in this teaching on the purpose and meaning of

Life. Thank you for thinking of me for all of eternity. Thank you for creating me as a unique, precious and unrepeatable manifestation of your Love. Thank you for counting me among your beloved children, and for giving me the Blessed Mother to be the perfect model for me to imitate in her relationships with you. I now ask Mary my Mother and my Guardian Angel to gather all the graces from the truth of this teaching; and please, Holy Spirit, seal them in my soul forever so that they may bear fruit in time and in eternity. Amen.

DAY THREE – Going Deeper with STMD

Is God calling you deeper? Following are ways to go deeper with Jesus, who calls you to see Him revealed in the Bible (Sacred Scripture), orthodox writings of the saints (faithful witness to Sacred Tradition) and the Catechism (Magisterium's faithful exposition of the Deposit of Faith)—STMD.

Jesus, I know You are the answer to all of my questions. Please reveal yourself to me in Sacred Scripture:

> *For all who are led by the Spirit of God are sons of God.*
> *For you did not receive the spirit of slavery to fall back*
> *into fear, but you have received a Spirit of sonship.*
> *When we cry, "Abba! Father!" it is the Spirit himself*
> *bearing witness with our spirit that we are children of*
> *God, and if children, then heirs, heirs of God and fellow*
> *heirs with Christ, provided we suffer with him in*
> *order that we may also be glorified with him*

(Romans 8:14-17).

As the Father has loved me, so have I loved you; abide in my love (John 15:9).

For the word of God is living and active, sharper than any two-edged sword, piercing to the division of soul and spirit, of joints and marrow, and discerning the thoughts and intentions of the heart (Hebrews 4:12).

Feel free to find these passages in your Bible and read them in context. You may even want to read them once silently and then out loud. Spend some time thinking about them, and then take them to prayer. It is always a good idea to memorize verses of Sacred Scripture and make them your own. This is just another way to know Jesus (Who is the Eternal Word) a little better.

Jesus, I know You are the answer to all of my questions. Please reveal yourself to me in the orthodox writings of the saints, which provide a faithful witness to Sacred Tradition.

We desire to imitate Mary to better understand how to fully and beautifully live an authentic Christian life. St. Gregory of Nyssa tells us that:

> "Since we who are called 'Christians' have been granted the honor of sharing this name, the greatest, the highest, the most sublime of all names, it follows that each of the titles that expresses its meaning should be clearly reflected in us. If we are not to lie when we call ourselves 'Christians', we must bear witness to it by our way

of living".[1]

You might want to know more about the saint who is quoted above. A Weekday Missal is a great place to start when you want to know more about certain saints. And there are many good resources on the internet and in the library about great saints.

Jesus, I know You are the answer to all of my questions. Please reveal yourself to me in the Magisterium's faithful exposition of the Deposit of Faith.

You can turn to the *Catechism of the Catholic Church*, number 2030:

> "It is in the Church, in communion with all the baptized, that the Christian fulfills his vocation. From the Church he receives the Word of God containing the teachings of 'the law of Christ.' From the Church he receives the grace of the sacraments that sustains him on the 'way.' From the Church he learns the *example of holiness* and recognizes its model and source in the all-holy Virgin Mary; he discerns it in the authentic witness of those who live it; he discovers it in the spiritual tradition and long history of the saints who have gone before him and whom the liturgy celebrates in the rhythms of the sanctoral cycle."

"Holy Church is our Mother, to feed us, rear us, and lead us to heaven." The treasures the Church has for us are never-ending, because the Source of all these treasures is God, Who is Infinite and

---

1   *Liturgy of the Hours*, Volume III, Page 392.

never gets tired of giving good gifts to His children. You may want to read more about the riches of the Church in Part Three of the *Catechism*, Life in Christ.

Use this space to write down any additional thoughts, prayers or epiphanies the Lord has given you during this first teaching in your spiritual formation:

Chapter Two

"How can I pray?"

Peaople are asking, "How can I pray?" The answer is: "Jesus."
When you pray the "Our Father," you are entering into the
perfect prayer of Jesus to the Father in the Holy Spirit. Let's
begin today by praying along with Jesus.

In the name of the Father and of the Son and of the Holy
Spirit. Amen.

Our Father who art in heaven, hallowed be Thy Name. Thy
Kingdom come. Thy will be done, on earth as it is in heaven.
Give us this day our daily bread, and forgive us our trespasses,
as we forgive those who trespass against us, and lead us not into
temptation, but deliver us from evil. Amen.

Our Lady of the Most Holy Trinity, pray for us.

In the name of the Father and of the Son and of the Holy
Spirit. Amen.

Prayer opens our minds and hearts to hear and understand God's
will in our lives. In prayer, God reveals His plan of Life and Love to us
and fills us with the graces and the blessings to be happy, holy, and

reach heaven. Prayer is essential to happiness and holiness. When we pray the Lord's Prayer along with Jesus, we claim the truth that God is "Our Father" and we are His children. We are reminded of how deeply He loves us and that we belong to Him, and that everything else in life is incidental.

Praying through Jesus, with Jesus, and in Jesus will deepen our understanding that God is Our Father; just like Our Lord said! It is through the Holy Spirit that we can cry out, "Abba, Father!" "Abba" is a term of deep, tender love and affection, like the word "Daddy." When we pray through, with, and in Jesus, we develop a relationship with God that is so intimate that we can call Him "Daddy." We could never earn such a tremendous privilege. The freedom to call the Father "Abba" is His gift to us, won by Our Lord Jesus Christ through the power of the Holy Spirit. What a tender, loving, and beautiful God we have!

In prayer we learn to humbly come before Our Father in heaven and trust Him. Once we understand (through the gift of faith) that God really is Our Father, we will discover new joys in prayer. We all enjoy spending time with those who truly love us—those who even treasure us—it makes us feel good. And there is no one who loves and treasures us more than God. If it is difficult for you to believe this, ask Our Blessed Mother to teach you. You can also ask her (and the whole company of heaven) to pray for you to deeply know God's love for you. Ask God for the gift of Faith so that you may know and believe in His incredible love. Once you understand God's supernatural, infinite love for you, you will desire to live God's perfect will for you in His Divine Plan of Love. You can learn how to do God's will from Our

Blessed Mother, beloved daughter of the Father. Mary always did God's will perfectly in that she did not sin. Her entire life was a prayer, for she continuously prayed. Our Lord instructs us to pray always and Our Lady (being the first and perfect disciple of Jesus) prayed always. She "prayed without ceasing." You may say, "How do I do that?" Good question.

Basics about Prayer

One way to pray without ceasing is to rise in the morning and say from your heart (because true prayer is always from the heart) the two greatest commandments: *I shall love the Lord my God with all my heart and all my soul and with my whole mind and with all my strength, and I shall love my neighbor as myself.* Then, from your heart you pray a morning offering. By saying a morning offering, you make everything in your day a prayer. There are many good morning offerings written. Here is one we recommend:

> *Oh Jesus, in union with Your most Precious Blood*
> *poured out on the Cross once and offered today at every*
> *Mass, I offer You today my prayers, works, joys, sorrows*
> *and sufferings for the praise of Your Holy Name and all*
> *the desires of your Sacred Heart, the Immaculate Heart*
> *of Mary and the Just Heart of Joseph, in reparation*
> *for sins, for the conversion of sinners, the union of all*
> *Christians and our final union with You in heaven.*

If you offer your whole day to God (everything—every beat of your heart, every breath you take, every step you make), you are praying without ceasing. This prayer is made in the united hearts of Jesus, Mary and Joseph. Because you are uniting with them, this prayer is an offering that is holy and acceptable to God. Would you like your whole day to be a prayer? It's simple! Start your day this way, and remember to frequently cover yourself with the virtues and merits of Jesus, Mary and Joseph.

Don't become so busy that you rush out into life and forget to pray. Prayer brings you the graces that you need to fulfill the plan of God for that day. We shouldn't rush out trying to fulfill our own plan for ourselves—that is vain, empty, meaningless and lonely. Rather, when we make our day a prayer, we find the graces, blessings, and strength to successfully handle the trials that arise in the day. Prayer is a beautiful way of life!

Prayer opens our hearts to the presence of God in our lives, helping us be mindful of the presence of God throughout our day. Prayer, when it comes from the heart, draws us into God's presence and helps us to know that Our Father in heaven is looking upon us with love. The highest form of prayer is the Holy Sacrifice of the Mass. We encourage all to participate in daily Mass, pray the Holy Rosary each day, participate in Eucharistic Adoration, pray Sacred Scripture through *Lectio Divina*, and regularly keep company with God, Our Lady, and all the Holy Angels and Saints. Prayer is a privilege and a joy as we keep company with God.

Prayer reveals the unique plan of God for your life. Remember to end your day by thanking God for all His gifts and then examining your conscience. Examine your thoughts and actions of the day and try to find any lack of virtue. Try to discover any moments when you were not open to God's free gift of grace in your life, and ask Him to forgive you and to help you do better tomorrow. God loves to forgive His children and to offer His strength in our weakness. Praying the Psalms (any Psalm will do) is an ancient practice and a great way to end your day. You may consider learning how to pray the Divine Office, also known as the Liturgy of the Hours. This is a beautiful way to join in the prayer of Jesus to the Father, in union with the whole Church. You can ask your pastor how to pray this way.

Remember, you were created by God as a unique, precious and unrepeatable manifestation of His Love. You are His beloved child and He longs to hear from you. He wants you to trust Him with the deepest desires of your heart. When you pray, you deepen the bond of love between yourself and God. Through prayer, you discover the unlimited love of God for you, and His purpose and meaning for your life. With Jesus, in the power of the Holy Spirit, you can go to the Father and *with confidence draw near to the throne of grace, that we may receive mercy and find grace to help in time of need (Hebrews 4:16).* Your Father loves you and He is waiting to hear from you. What are you waiting for? Don't wait, let's pray!

Thank you Father, Son, and Holy Spirit. Thank you for making me. Thank you for wanting to spend time with me. Thank you for loving me. Amen.

DAY ONE – Praying with Mary

Give yourself some time to just sit at Our Lady's feet. Give her the time to speak to your heart as you begin to truly know her as your dear Mother. After a little quiet time, you may wish to pray this lovely prayer:

A Child's Prayer to Mary

Dear Mother of Jesus, look down upon me as I say my prayers
slowly at my Mother's knee.
I love thee, O Lady, and please will thou bring all little children to
Jesus our King. Amen.
O beautiful Lady, clothed in blue, help me to know, love and serve
God by telling me what to do. Amen.

Ask yourself if you, like Mary, take the time to "ponder" the things of God in your heart. Ponder the following truth:

- As Our Lady consented to the will of God with her whole being in her "Fiat!" the greatest miracle in the history of mankind occurred—the Incarnation.

Our Lady demonstrates through her "Fiat!" that she had a perfect disposition for prayer. We want to imitate her, so we need to ask ourselves:

- How do I make myself ready for prayer?

- Do I set aside a specific time(s) for prayer?

- Is prayer a priority for me, or do I just get to it when I can?

- Do I enter into prayer with proper reverence and respect for the One to whom I am addressing?

- Does my bodily posture or demeanor aide in my prayer? Does such a thing even matter?

- Am I easily distracted during prayer or am I resolute?

• Do I spend time listening as well as talking in prayer, and do I humbly wait on the Lord for His response?

• And finally, the most important question of all: How badly do I want to pray? How intense is my longing for communication and union with the One who created me? Do I long to participate in His work of prayer?

Each day look carefully at the list of questions above. *Choose the question that speaks most profoundly to your heart and take it to prayer.* Enter into prayer asking Our Lady to give you Her Heart to seek the will of the Father and to be pleasing to Him alone. You may look at a different question each day, or the same one all week. Don't give up praying over that question until the Holy Spirit reveals the Wisdom of God to you.

We are reminded by St. Teresa of Avila: "When we have decided to give anything—such as this slight effort of recollection—to Him who has given us so much, and who is continually giving, it would be wrong for us not to be entirely resolute in doing so and to act like a person who lends something and expects to get it back again." *Spend time in prayer each day.*

DAY TWO – Praying in Jesus

No one has ever prayed with the beauty and intensity of Jesus. The disciples were men of prayer, but they also recognized something "more" in the prayer of Jesus, and this is what led them to beg Him, *"Teach us how to pray ...."* Jesus prayed the way He did because of one thing—the one thing that matters—Love. The Love of the Most

Holy Trinity is so beautiful, so intense, and so mighty that words can never begin to describe it. Jesus was driven to pray from a perfect, burning, and never-ending Love—a Love that we can pray for, too. God is waiting to give it to us, but we need to ask Him for it! We have to pray to pray!

Another Point to Ponder

When you want to pray, you'll pray. And there aren't any tricks. If you want to pray, you'll pray. And you won't look it up in a book. You'll pray. And if you know the presence of the Lord in your own soul, you'll praise God because you'll realize that you're not worthy. And you'll know the power of the presence of the merciful God, and you'll pray, you'll just pray. And so when we talk about prayer we are reflecting on something that's going on. It really isn't up to us whether or not we're going to pray, as though prayer were something we start. It's up to us whether or not we're going to agree to pray. The Spirit of God lives in us. The Spirit of God is always crying out, "Abba, Father." The Spirit of God is always "returning" to the Father and it is up to us whether or not we want to agree with that.[2]

Ask yourself if you have really begged God (from the bottom of your heart) for the gift of charity and the gift of prayer. If you haven't, what are you waiting for? Don't wait any longer, let's pray:

Dear God, I beg you to give me the gift of charity and the gift of

---

2   Fr. Francis Martin, "Teach Us to Pray," *Magnificat*, October 2008, pg. 119.

prayer. Teach me how to pray, Holy Spirit! I want to reach the heart of my Father in You, My Faithful Advocate: please help me to pray as I ought. Blessed Mother, please beg the Blessed Trinity for me for the gift of prayer. I want to pray and to ponder in my heart as you do. Let me be found pleasing in Your sight, dear Lord; let me lift up my heart, mind and soul to you and give you all you deserve, all of me in my prayer. I ask all of this in the Holy Name of Jesus, in the power of the Holy Spirit, to the glory of God the Father. Amen.

DAY THREE – Going Deeper with STMD

Is God calling you deeper? Following are ways to go deeper with Jesus, who calls you to see Him revealed in the Bible (Sacred Scripture), orthodox writings of the saints (faithful witness to Sacred Tradition) and the Catechism (Magisterium's faithful exposition of the Deposit of Faith)—STMD.

Jesus, I know You are the answer to all of my questions. Please reveal yourself to me in Sacred Scripture:

Scripture to Claim

Rejoice always, pray constantly, give thanks in all circumstances; for this is the will of God in Christ Jesus for you (1 Thessalonians 5:16-18).

But when you pray, go into your room and shut the door, and pray to your Father who is in secret; and your Father who sees in secret will reward you (Matthew 6:6).

Ask, and it will be given you; seek, and you will find; knock, and it will be opened to you. For every one who

asks receives, and he who seeks finds, and to him who
knocks it will be opened (Matthew 7:7-8).

Feel free to find these passages in your Bible and read them in context. You may even want to read them once silently and then out loud. Spend some time thinking about them, and then take them to prayer. It is always a good idea to memorize verses of Sacred Scripture and make them your own. This is just another way to know Jesus a little better.

Jesus, I know You are the answer to all of my questions. Please reveal yourself to me in the orthodox writings of the saints, which provide a faithful witness to Sacred Tradition.

Noted in number 2558 of the *Catechism of the Catholic Church*, St. Thérèse of Lisieux says:

> "For me, prayer is a surge of the heart; it is a simple
> look turned toward heaven, it is a cry of recognition
> and of love, embracing both trial and joy." (*Manuscrits*
> *autobiographiques*, C 25r)

Certainly, we can learn much from this Doctor of the Church, who prayed so well because she loved so deeply. Take the time to pray to St. Thérèse and ask her to show you how to love God more deeply and perfectly so that you can pray from deep within your heart. She is sure to hear you and to help you love Jesus more perfectly.

You might want to know more about the saint who is quoted above. A Weekday Missal is a great place to start when you want to know more about certain saints. And there are many good resources on the internet and in the library about great saints.

Jesus, I know You are the answer to all of my questions. Please reveal yourself to me in the Magisterium's faithful exposition of the Deposit of Faith.

You can turn to the *Catechism of the Catholic Church*, number 2567:

> *God calls man first.* Man may forget his Creator or hide far from his face; he may run after idols or accuse the deity of having abandoned him; yet the living and true God tirelessly calls each person to that mysterious encounter known as prayer. In prayer, the faithful God's initiative of love always comes first; our own first step is always a response.

Part Four of the *Catechism* is entitled, Christian Prayer, and offers an entire wealth of knowledge on this most important relationship with our God. Please take the time to read what the Church teaches about prayer in the *Catechism.* You will be blessed and enriched by the wisdom written there.

Use this space to write down any additional thoughts, prayers or epiphanies the Lord has given you during this teaching in your spiritual formation:

Chapter Three

"In Whose image and likeness have I been created?"

People are asking, "In Whose image and likeness have I been created?" The answer is: God, who is Father, Son and Holy Spirit. And Jesus, God the Son, is "the image of the invisible God, the firstborn of all creation" (Colossians 1:15). Let's turn to Him now by praying the "perfect prayer" along with Jesus, the "Our Father":

In the name of the Father and of the Son and of the Holy Spirit. Amen.

Our Father who art in heaven, hallowed be Thy Name. Thy Kingdom come. Thy will be done, on earth as it is in heaven. Give us this day our daily bread, and forgive us our trespasses, as we forgive those who trespass against us, and lead us not into temptation, but deliver us from evil. Amen.

Our Lady of the Most Holy Trinity, pray for us.

In the name of the Father and of the Son and of the Holy Spirit. Amen.

The Most Holy Trinity (Father, Son and Holy Spirit) wants you to understand that you are created in the image and likeness of God. This is necessary because in order to move forward in your relationship with the Trinity, you must recognize and claim your dignity.

There are seven ways that we can say are consequences of *both* our being made in the image and likeness of God and our being disciples of Christ. The acronym we can use to remember them is "KCGLGDC." "K" stands for our capacity to know God (cf. *CCC* 356), which increases markedly by virtue of our becoming His disciples, beginning in the sacrament of Baptism when we receive the theological virtues of faith, hope and love (*CCC* 1266). "C" stands for helping communicate God's life to others through our witness as Catholics. When God communicates, he provides life-giving truth, all of which is ultimately designed to lead us into right relationship with Him. As Catholics, we should emulate God and help lead others into the eternally life-giving communion of the Trinity.

"G" stands for goals, meaning that we respond to God's goals for our life and those of others with whom we interact. "L" stands for love. We are to make love visible, just as Jesus makes God visible. We're going to learn how to make God's love visible, drawing from His infinite love. The second "G" is gifts. We identify the gifts that God has given us in abundance, with a good measure, pressed down and flowing over. These gifts are given to us to give to others. Too many people use them only for themselves. But God gave them to us to give to others and when we share them, the blessings and joy that come are amazing. "D" stands for destiny. We all have a destiny, a purpose and meaning of life. The plan of communion—that is our destiny. Speaking of which, the last "C" is community. We are all created for community because God Himself (Father, Son and Holy Spirit) is a community, a perfect communion. We are created for community. That is why God placed us in a family when we were born, to learn how to live in a community. God wants us to know the joy of living in communion in our own community, similar to the Trinity, in whose image and likeness we are created. Ultimately, God wants us to enjoy heavenly communion with Him and each other.

In Genesis, the very first book of Sacred Scripture (chapter 1, verse 26), *Then God said, "Let us make man in our image, after our likeness…."* Let us, Father, Son and Holy Spirit, make man in our image and likeness—one of the most profound statements in all of Sacred Scripture, right at the very beginning. Why did the God of the universe choose to create us in His image and likeness? So that we can enter into a perfect relationship with Him called "communion." God is perfect communion in Himself—One God in Three Divine Persons: Father, Son and Holy Spirit. He wants us to enjoy communion with Him. We are created in the image and likeness of God to live with Him eternally, to live in communion with Him forever.

You have learned that you are a unique, precious and unrepeatable manifestation of God's goodness. There is no one in the entire universe exactly like you. God made you for Himself out of love, and He desires communion with you. Have you ever considered that no one else in the world can have exactly the same relationship with God as you? If you decide to withhold your friendship from God—to distance yourself from Him—no one else in the world can take your place in His Heart. That is a startling thought. To God, you are a gift that cannot be replaced, duplicated or exchanged. In fact, in the

Gospel of John 17:24, Jesus says this about us:

> *"Father, I desire that they also, whom thou hast given me, may be with me where I am, to behold my glory which thou hast given me in thy love for me before the foundation of the world."*

Now, THAT is the TRUTH! Jesus says here that you have been given to Him by the Father. Do you realize what that means you are? It means you are a one-of-a-kind gift, given to Jesus by His Father. Not only does Jesus say that you are a gift to Him, but also that He wants you to be with Him. He wants to show you things. He wants you to see His glory. He wants you to know that you are also loved eternally. Again we can be so encouraged by Our Lady! His prayer was realized in her Assumption (her body and soul taken into heaven). She is now in heaven with Him, seeing his glory while dwelling with Him in eternal love. Don't think for even a moment, "Yes, but that was only for her." Her assumption (body and soul) is a unique privilege reserved for her; that is true. But a day is coming when all of us who are faithful will see Him face-to-face. When that day comes, we should be prepared to meet Him with full knowledge of who we are in His sight. Take a moment to ponder that truth.

Let's begin to see ourselves through His eyes. Please read each of the following statements paraphrased from Holy Scripture, one-by-one. They are each very short but powerful truths that Jesus has spoken about you. After you read each one, close your eyes and look with your heart into the face of Jesus. See Him and listen to His words. Ask Our Lady to approach Him with you. In essence, these are His Words to you:

You are My child (I John 3:1).

I have chosen you (John 7:6).

I call you friends (John 15:15).

You are a gift to me (John 17:24).

Child, chosen, friend, gift—this is who you are. Now is the time to start believing His truth about yourself. "In Whose image and likeness have I been created?" "Jesus."

DAY ONE –

Reflecting with Mary on the Image and Likeness of God

We want to live the Truth of being created in God's image and likeness. Our Lady lived it with great faith and blessedness. She lived this truth so profoundly that she gave birth to Him who is Truth. We want to imitate Our Lady in all things, and we begin here. You can't travel any further until you really believe that you are an image and likeness of God. Then you must be sure of who you are in His sight.

Mary fully represents the perfect human example of the seven realities of image and likeness. She was able to:

- **K**now herself

- **C**ommunicate herself

- Set **G**oals

- Make her **L**ove visible

- Use her **G**ifts for the good of all

- Take hold of her **D**estiny

- Live in **C**ommunity

Note: If you are interested in another fun way to remember these seven aspects of being created in the image and likeness of God, you can go to our website and download a song from our SOLT Kids! Program entitled "KCGLGDC." It has a catchy little tune that will help commit these aspects to memory.

Take some time to quietly contemplate the following:

- What traits of Our Lady show her unique way of living the knowledge of being created in the image and likeness of God?

- What is the most difficult obstacle in your life to living this truth that you are created in the image and likeness of God?

DAY TWO –

Reflecting with Jesus on the Image and Likeness of God

To become like Jesus, we must believe that we are God's choice. We are His work of art. Jesus, being the only Son of God, absolutely knew His worth in the eyes of His Father in heaven. When we present this idea to little children, they almost always believe and understand this truth. But we, who have a few battle scars, may not. Please read through this children's poem from our SOLT Kids! Program on the image and likeness of God:

His Work of Art

I know that I'm a child of God, my Father lives above.

I know that I'm a child of God, created in His love.

The Father, Son and Spirit hold me within their heart.

God's image and God's likeness make me His work of art.

And calling to him a child, he put him in the midst of them, and said, "Truly, I say to you, unless you turn and become like children, you will never enter the kingdom of heaven. Whoever humbles himself like this child, he is the greatest in the kingdom of heaven" (*Matthew 18:2-4*). Jesus taught us to call God "Father," so we are His children. God wants us to depend upon Him completely, just like a little child. When we fully understand that God is Our Father and that we are His beloved children, we can be certain that He is delighted when we rely on Him for everything. We should want to become just like our "Abba," showing that we are made in his image and likeness by our kindness, love and good deeds. People who meet us should be able to see the "family resemblance," knowing that we are children of God by the beauty of our lives.

So how can we become like Jesus? We can start by believing that we are God's choice. Many of us have seen the pro-life bumper sticker that states "It's a Child, Not a Choice." We should print some new ones that we can paste on our foreheads saying "I am a child by God's choice." God has chosen you. He has called you by name. He has a plan and a purpose for you. He wants to set the world ablaze with love through you. He wants to love His people through you. He wants you to take hold of the destiny He has given you. He wants to live in communion with you. He wants you to know that He is passionately and unreservedly in love with you, and that He will pursue you and woo you until your dying breath. He wants all of you because He chose you, and He created you for Himself—in His image and likeness, so that you can love Him not only now but forevermore.

Do you want to expand your relationship with God? Do you want to become like Jesus? Then believe that you are His choice, made in His image and likeness. That is the truth about you—claim it!

Reflect on the following:

- There is a great and blessed responsibility that comes with knowing yourself as a child of God. As you lay hold of your destiny, teach this truth to others and gather more souls into the Kingdom of God. This is a truth that can set people free.

- Remember—Our Lord was a Man of action! He made his Love visible. To become like Him, you have to do that, too. Think of ways that you can make your love visible today. Make it your aim to show your love to one who might not expect it.

- How will this knowledge that I am a true child of God shift me into action in my relationships (both with self and others)?

Let us pray:

Dear Father, Son and Holy Spirit, thank you for creating me in your image and likeness as a unique, precious and unrepeatable manifestation of your goodness. Thank you for revealing the truth to me, that I am loved and known by You in a unique and personal way. Please seal all the graces associated with this new knowledge in my heart, and help me to share it with those you bring into my life. I give you all praise and glory for creating me to live in perfect love and communion with you forever. I love you, Lord. Amen.

DAY THREE – Going Deeper with STMD

Is God calling you deeper? Following are ways to go deeper with Jesus, who calls you to see Him revealed in the Bible (Sacred Scripture), orthodox writings of the saints (faithful witness to Sacred Tradition) and the Catechism (Magisterium's faithful exposition of the Deposit of Faith)—STMD.

Jesus, I know You are the answer to all of my questions. Please reveal yourself to me in Sacred Scripture:

> *God created man in his own image, in the image of God he created him, male and female he created them (Genesis 1:27).*

> *"You did not choose me, but I chose you and appointed you that you should go and bear fruit and that your fruit should abide; so that whatever you ask the Father in my name, he may give it to you" (John 15:16).*

Feel free to find these passages in your Bible and read them in context. You may even want to read them once silently and then out loud. Spend some time thinking about them, and then take them to prayer. It is always a good idea to memorize verses of Sacred Scripture and make them your own. This is just another way to know Jesus (Who is the Eternal Word) a little better.

Jesus, I know You are the answer to all of my questions. Please reveal yourself to me in the orthodox writings of the saints, which provide a faithful witness to Sacred Tradition.

We read in the *Catechism of the Catholic Church,* number 358:

"God created everything for man, (cf. *Gaudium et spes* 12§1; 24§3; 39§1) but man in turn was created to serve and love God and to offer all creation back to him:

> What is it that is about to be created that enjoys such honor? It is man—that great and wonderful living creature, more precious in the eyes of God than all other creatures! For him the heavens and the earth, the sea and all the rest of creation exist. God attached so much importance to his salvation that he did not spare his own Son for the sake of man. Nor does he ever cease to work, trying every possible means, until he has raised man up to himself and made him sit at his right hand. (St. John Chrysostom, *In Gen. Sermo* II; 1: PG 54, 597D-588A)"

You might want to know more about the saint who is quoted above. A Weekday Missal is a great place to start when you want to know more about certain saints. And there are many good resources on the internet and in the library about great saints.

Jesus, I know You are the answer to all of my questions. Please reveal yourself to me in the Magisterium's faithful exposition of the Deposit of Faith.

You can turn to the *Catechism of the Catholic Church*, number 357:

> Being in the image of God the human individual possesses the dignity of a person, who is not just something,

but someone. He is capable of self-knowledge, of self-possession and of freely giving himself and entering into communion with other persons. And he is called by grace to a covenant with his Creator, to offer him a response of faith and love that no other creature can give in his stead.

Part One of the *Catechism*, The Profession of Faith, begins a teaching on Man created in the image and likeness of God. To gain even more insight into this awesome gift of Truth, you may want to read numbers 355-421.

Use this space to write down any additional thoughts, prayers or epiphanies the Lord has given you during this teaching in your spiritual formation:

Chapter Four

"How do I live the Universal Call to Holiness?"

People are asking, "How do I live the universal call to holiness?" The answer is: "Jesus." Let us begin now by praying the "perfect prayer" along with Jesus, the "Our Father":

In the name of the Father and of the Son and of the Holy Spirit. Amen.

Our Father who art in heaven, hallowed be Thy Name. Thy Kingdom come. Thy will be done, on earth as it is in heaven. Give us this day our daily bread, and forgive us our trespasses, as we forgive those who trespass against us, and lead us not into temptation, but deliver us from evil. Amen.

Our Lady of the Most Holy Trinity, pray for us.

In the name of the Father and of the Son and of the Holy Spirit. Amen.

You must have noticed by now that we begin each new teaching with the Lord's Prayer, known as the "Our Father." This perfect prayer helps us to understand ourselves as true children of God, just like Jesus (our Savior and Brother) and Mary (our mother and sister). The

"Our Father" contains all of the petitions that we need to live a holy way of life. When you pray the "Our Father" slowly, with the heart of Our Blessed Mother as a trusting child, you discover that God wants His name to be holy in us. We are God's children, and He has given us His family name...*and holy is His name.* In the Holy Sacrifice of the Mass we proclaim: *Holy, holy, holy Lord, God of power and might, heaven and earth are full of your glory. Hosanna in the highest. Blessed is He who comes in the name of the Lord. Hosanna in the highest.* Blessed are we who come in the name of the Lord, and holy is His name. Holiness is for everybody. As we pray the "Our Father" prayer, we trust God. We seek to do His will. He gives us the grace to have His kingdom come as He gives us His daily bread, the Eucharist. And He asks us to be a forgiving people, to overcome temptation, and to leave evil. Holiness is contained in the "Our Father" prayer. Holiness is in our relationship with God the Father, Son, and Holy Spirit. We are called! Sacred Scripture tells us to be holy as God is holy. And that is the answer to what holiness is—living as Jesus lives.

Sainthood: God's Plan for You

God's plan is for you to become a saint. This reality will continually be presented in this program to help you realize that you are created to be a saint. Become the saint that you are created to be—claim it. It is a holy desire. It is not prideful to try to become a saint. The enemy will whisper, "Oh, that's pride," because he is terrified of the saints. But you are created to be a saint. You are simply responding to God's plan. It is a holy desire to become a saint, and that is why you are baptized—to live the life of Christ, the Holy One of God.

Sanctity is not just for the priests. It is not just for the sisters. It is for you, and it is for all. Some people say, "I have never heard of such a thing, Father. I thought holiness was just for the chosen." But the reality is that we are all chosen and we are all called. That is why you are reading this book. God and Our Blessed Mother want you to know that you are called to be holy. Remember the three "H's:" Holiness, Happiness and Heaven. We keep those three "H's" connected because true happiness is the fruit of holiness, and a holy, happy life will bring us to heaven.

Living Your Baptism

You are called to be holy by virtue of your baptism. Being baptized into Christ means that you are to live the life of Christ. Living the life of Christ means that you will be holy. Our Lady will teach you how to live the life of Christ, and to radiate the Trinitarian life of Christ to others. You received this Trinitarian life in your Baptism. You received the life of the Father, the Son, and the Holy Spirit in your Baptism. In the Baptismal Rite, we use the Trinitarian form where the priest or deacon pours water over the child's head and says, "I baptize you in the name of the Father and of the Son and of the Holy Spirit." You become a child of the Father, a disciple of the Son, and a temple of the Holy Spirit. Actually, you are baptized into the light of Christ, in whom we live and move and have our being. We no longer live for ourselves because we live in Christ—we live a holy life. We belong to God. We love God above all things and we seek to do His holy will. Our Lady teaches us to live this life of Christ.

Christ's life is Trinitarian, as he is in perfect communion with the Father and the Holy Spirit. As a perfect Son, he also loves and honors His mother, whom he gives to us as our spiritual mother. In the Society of Our Lady of the Most Holy Trinity, we thus have a Trinitarian-Marian spirituality. Some people want to argue about the role of the Blessed Virgin Mary, but it all comes down to this: She is loved by Jesus, she is loved by the Father, and she is loved by the Holy Spirit. We should love her, too. All she wants is for us to live our Baptism in Christ. She is the good mother of Christ and a good mother always loves to bring forth her child. With a Father's heart, God gives us a beautiful mother to help us live a holy way of life. In Our Lady's community, our spirituality is to *Imitate Mary, Become like Jesus, and Live for the Triune God.* This is holiness! It is living our Baptism. We live the life of God Himself. God freely gives all of us this life in our Baptism.

All of the theology of John Paul the Great (our Holy Father who lived a holy life) was about calling people back to their Baptism. If you are living your Baptism, you are living a holy way of life. But most people don't know how to live their Baptism because they think that Baptism is only about washing away original sin. Certainly, that takes place. Certainly, it is God's incredible gift of redemption, won for us on the Cross. In Baptism, original sin is washed away; but we still carry the consequence of original sin within us, our fallen human nature.

When you sin, you fail to live your Baptism. When you do not see yourself as a "sent" person, you lose sight of God's plan in your life. Sin is when you do things below your dignity. But Jesus is waiting for you. The Father is waiting for you. The Holy Spirit is waiting for you. The Father talks to you about His plan for you through the priest in the Sacrament of Penance and Reconciliation (more commonly called "Confession"). Basically, sin is when you fail to do the will of God. The will of God is His plan of love for you. The Father wants you to live your Baptism to live the life of Christ. When you sin, you are not living your Baptism and you are not living the life of Christ.

Let us look at the positive side as well. In Baptism you became a child of the Father, a disciple of Jesus, and a temple of His Holy Spirit—you became a member of the Church. You were given Our Blessed Mother as your mother. You were anointed as priest, prophet and king—priest in the common priesthood of all the faithful. (All the baptized share in the common priesthood. Ordained Priests belong to the Ministerial Priesthood in Holy Orders.)

All of us are to offer sacrifice (like a Priest) in the common priesthood of our Baptism. We are to be prophets who proclaim the Truth that sets people free. We proclaim Jesus Christ who is the Truth. We live in a world where people try to make the truth relative to themselves. We call this "relativism," and it comes from our enemy. Truth is not relative to any human person. The Truth is Jesus Christ, who says, *"I am the Way, the Truth and the Life."* The Truth is the same yesterday, today and forever. This is why the Church is not blown around by the winds of political correctness. That is not what the Church is about. The Church is about Jesus—it is about the Truth.

The Church is here to proclaim Jesus Christ and to give Jesus Christ to the world. And that is what you are to do in living out your Baptism and the universal call to holiness. Because you received Jesus Christ, you are to give Jesus Christ. And that is a holy way of life. The answer to all the questions that burn in your heart is "Jesus." By virtue of your Baptism, since you were anointed priest, prophet and king, you should give Jesus to everyone you meet.

Basically, we do Our Father's will and we love God above all things for Himself. This is the key to holiness Again, the Holy Spirit is "the origin and source of our sanctification" or holiness (*CCC* 190), and Our Lady teaches us how to live a holy life (*CCC* 2030). She will be happy to teach you in particular.

Let me share a secret with you. As an ordained Catholic Priest, the Father sends me people to serve. I ask the Father to help me fulfill His plan for this person and the Father says, "Give them Jesus, my Son." I say, "Yes, I will give them Jesus." He sends me another person and I ask Him to help me fulfill His plan for this person and He says, "Give them Jesus, my Son." He sends me another person and I say, "Father, help me fulfill Your plan for this person," and He says, "Give them Jesus Christ, my Son." Finally, I started to catch on. My whole life is giving people Jesus. I have learned that the best way to give people Jesus is to give them Our Blessed Mother because she knows Jesus intimately. Furthermore, Mary, our mother, loves us perfectly.

"How do I live the universal call to holiness?" "Jesus."

DAY ONE – Imitating Mary in Her Call to Holiness

Mary always points to her Son, Jesus. She can never be accused of pointing to herself. She lived a life of holiness and beauty in the sight of God and man. Her last recorded words in Sacred Scripture are from the Wedding Feast at Cana. You may want to read the entire account of this first public miracle of Jesus in the Gospel of John, chapter 2.

Upon noticing that the wine had run out, Mary spoke to her Son

Jesus and consequently directed the servants, *"Do whatever he tells you."* The servants proceeded as directed and the wedding banquet was saved by the miracle of Jesus. As we go deeper into accepting the call to holiness, we must come to embrace several realizations:

First: Our Lady knows our call to holiness and brought us here.

Regarding the Wedding Feast at Cana, in his *Sunday Sermons* (#48), St. Alphonsus Liguori shows us that no one asked the Blessed Mother to intervene. She notices that the wine has run out and "it stirs her to act as intercessor and ask her Son for the miracle, even though no one asks her to." What a joy! Our Blessed Mother (your mother in heaven), recognizing your call to holiness, has brought you here. Before you knew it, she had interceded on your behalf already. We can therefore continue to move forward in full confidence that she will guide us and intercede for us on this journey. At the end of this "call to holiness" teaching we hear the Father say, "God loves you; receive His mercy. Turn to Our Lady and ask her to help you. Our mother is waiting for you; call out her name: 'Mary, Mary, my mother, help me to live my life as a child of God. Help me live my Baptism. Guide me to become the saint I was created to be."

Second: Her direction is simple and clear.

Our Lady directs the servants to *"do whatever He tells you."* Mary knows who her Son is. She knows that all things are possible with Him. She recognizes His Divinity and Providence over all things. She doesn't tell the servants *how* to do it, just to do it. She points us to her Son, to His Divinity and Providence. He has given us the gift of the Church and through her the gift of Himself. In formation, we discover that the spirit of the world is confusing, but the Church is clear. As we move forward in formation, the teachings of the Church will unfold like a beautiful flower. Through her wisdom and gifts, we are greatly aided in living a life of holiness.

Third: The servants obey and everyone is blessed.

Jesus tells the servants to fill six jugs with water. He tells us in the Gospel of Matthew, *"You, therefore, must be perfect, as your heavenly Father is perfect" (Matthew 5:48).* And He gives us all that we need to fulfill this command in our Baptism and in the life of the Church.

The Call to Holiness

The Church encourages us in our call to holiness in *Lumen Gentium* from the Second Vatican Council:

> "…all Christ's faithful, **whatever be the conditions, duties and circumstances** of their daily lives—and indeed through all these—will daily increase in holiness, if they receive all things with faith from the hand of their heavenly Father and if they cooperate with the divine will. In this temporal service, they will manifest to all men the love with which God loved the world" (Lumen Gentium, number 41, emphasis added).

Let us first review this phrase, "whatever are the conditions, duties and circumstances." This is an important part of the call to holiness. It means that the Church recognizes that God wants us to constantly live the call to holiness at all times. We can't wait for this or that to happen. We must be careful not to say, "Well, I'll start growing in holiness after I get that promotion at work," or "There's too much going on right now; I need to catch up first," or "If only I was married, then I would really work at living a holy life." No, no, no. God chose you now and He means now. It also means that we can't say, "Well, I'm not a priest" or "I'm busy with no extra time." God knows our time. He creates it and controls it.

Reflect on the following:

- What am I already doing to respond to the universal call to holiness? (For example: Do I participate in Mass every Sunday and Holy Day of Obligation? Do I participate in daily Mass regularly? Have I recently received the wonderful gift of the Sacrament of Penance and Reconciliation?)

- Jesus told the servants to fill six jugs with water. He tells us in Matthew, *"You, therefore, must be perfect, as your heavenly Father is perfect" (Matthew 5:48).* And He gives us all that we need to fulfill this command through our Baptism and the life of the Church. Had you ever heard before that you are called to be a saint? How does this call challenge you?

DAY TWO – Becoming Like Jesus in His Call to Holiness

Consider writing out the following statement in your prayer journal and signing it:

Jesus, I hear Your call to live a life of holiness in Your Word and through Your Church. Similar to Mother Mary, I say "Yes!" to this call, with a firm resolve to embrace that which pleases You and amend that which offends You. Jesus, I trust in You. Our Lady of the Most Holy Trinity, pray for me.

_____

Signed   Date

This week make some small, yet OBVIOUS, changes that will remind you to continue answering the Call to Holiness. When you recognize the reminder, say "Jesus, I Trust in You!"

- Change the ring tones on your home phone and/or cell phone.

- Move your toothbrush to another location.

- Ask a friend or family member to make a special prayer for you during the next seven months. Know that you have the prayers of the priests, religious and lay members of the Society of the Most Holy Trinity.

Let us pray:

Dear Father, Son and Holy Spirit, I want to respond to Your call of holiness. Help me to do what you would have me to do. Help me to pray. Give me strength through the Eucharist to live the life of Christ. Father, may your will be done in me. I ask all of this in the Name of Jesus and through the power of the Holy Spirit Who dwells within me. Amen.

DAY THREE – Going Deeper with STMD

Is God calling you deeper? Following are ways to go deeper with Jesus, who calls you to see Him revealed in the Bible (Sacred Scripture), orthodox writings of the saints (faithful witness to Sacred Tradition) and the Catechism (Magisterium's faithful exposition of the Deposit of Faith)—STMD.

Jesus, I know You are the answer to all of my questions. Please reveal yourself to me in Sacred Scripture:

"Do whatever He tells you" (John 2:5).

"You, therefore, must be perfect, as your heavenly Father is perfect" (Matthew 5:48).

Feel free to find these passages in your Bible and read them in context. You may even want to read them once silently and then out loud. Spend some time thinking about them, and then take them to prayer. It is always a good idea to memorize verses of Sacred Scripture and make them your own. This is just another way to know Jesus (Who is the Eternal Word) a little better.

Jesus, I know You are the answer to all of my questions. Please reveal yourself to me in the orthodox writings of the saints, which provide a faithful witness to Sacred Tradition.

We read this beautiful prayer in the writings of St. Ignatius of Loyola:

> "Take, O Lord, and receive my entire liberty, my memory, my understanding, and my whole will. All that I am and all that I possess, You have given me; I surrender it all to You to be disposed of according to Your will. Give me only Your love and Your grace; with these I will be rich enough, and will desire nothing more. Amen."

You might want to know more about the saint who is quoted above. A Weekday Missal is a great place to start when you want to know more about certain saints. And there are many good resources on the internet and in the library about great saints.

Jesus, I know You are the answer to all of my questions. Please reveal yourself to me in the Magisterium's faithful exposition of the Deposit of Faith.

You can turn to the *Catechism of the Catholic Church*, number 2015:

> The way of perfection passes by the way of the Cross. There is no holiness without renunciation and spiritual battle. (Cf. 2 Tim 4) Spiritual progress entails the ascesis and mortification that gradually lead to living in the peace and joy of the Beatitudes:

> He who climbs never stops going from beginning to beginning, through beginnings that have no end. He never stops desiring what he already knows (St. Gregory of Nyssa, *Hom. in Cant.* 8:PG 44, 941C).

Part Three of the *Catechism,* Life in Christ, will help you understand even more about the Universal Call to Holiness. You may wish to read numbers 2012-2016 in particular.

Use this space to write down any additional thoughts, prayers or epiphanies the Lord has given you during this teaching in your spiritual formation:

Chapter Five

"What is a Rule of Life?"

P eople are asking, "What is a Rule of Life?" The answer is: "Jesus." If you live the Life of Christ, you will automatically be living the perfect "Rule of Life." But most of you are not quite sure how to do that, so we will guide you through the creation of your very own "Rule." Prayer is what your Rule of Life is all about, so let's begin now by praying the "perfect prayer" along with Jesus, the "Our Father:"

In the name of the Father and of the Son and of the Holy Spirit. Amen.

Our Father who art in heaven, hallowed be Thy Name. Thy Kingdom come. Thy will be done, on earth as it is in heaven. Give us this day our daily bread, and forgive us our trespasses, as we forgive those who trespass against us, and lead us not into temptation, but deliver us from evil. Amen.

Our Lady of the Most Holy Trinity, pray for us.

In the name of the Father and of the Son and of the Holy Spirit. Amen.

Then God said, "Let us make man in our image, after our likeness; and let them have dominion over the fish of the sea, and over the birds of the air, and over the cattle, and over all the earth, and over every creeping thing that creeps upon the earth" (Genesis 1:26).

God created this world with order and He desires that our lives and our world be ordered by Love. We all live with a certain amount of order in our lives. We rise at certain times, we eat at certain times, and we dress according to the seasons. These habits are necessary to order our normal, everyday lives. But what do you do to order your spiritual life? Do you participate in Mass at least on Sundays and Holy Days of Obligation, begin your day with a prayer, say grace before meals, and pray for special intentions? This is all good; but in this Lay Formation Program, we desire to answer the call to holiness so we want more!

John Paul II the Great reminds us that the gift of holiness is offered to all the baptized. "But the gift (of holiness) in turn becomes a task, which must shape the whole of the Christian life."[3] "All the Christian faithful, of whatever state or rank, are called to the fullness of the Christian life and to the perfection of charity."[4] This holy Pope continues to encourage us, "It is clear, however, that the paths to holiness are personal and call for a genuine 'training in holiness', adapted to peoples' needs."[5]

Have you ever thought of being trained to grow in holiness? To

3   Pope John Paul II, *Novo Millenio Inuente*, No. 30.
4   *Lumen Gentium*, No. 40.
5   Pope John Paul II, *Novo Millenio Inuente*, No. 31.

assist our "training in holiness," we are going to discern a personal Rule of Life with attention to our spiritual life, including our prayer life. When we want to get our bodies in shape, we develop a plan for physical exercise. When we want to get our spiritual lives in shape, we develop a Rule of Life.

The importance of a Rule of Life was witnessed by St. Benedict, who was born in the year 480 into a wealthy family in Nursia, Italy. Benedict was given the opportunity for higher education in Rome. But, disturbed by the self-indulgent atmosphere in Rome, he gave up his education and his entire inheritance to begin a lifelong spiritual journey. His desire for God eventually led to the beginning of monastic life. Benedict developed a "Holy Rule" because he recognized that a person's little daily choices ultimately determine the basic orientation of one's whole life. The intention of his Rule was to assist the monks in choosing Christ, day by day and moment by moment. Try not to think of it as a "rule" (in a negative light) but rather as a "guide" to holiness and happiness. Remember the teaching in the chapter on the Purpose and Meaning of Life, "Holiness is basically doing God's will and loving God for Himself above all things." We will help you discern a simple rule of life to order your path to holiness.

Let's examine some practical and spiritual goals of a Rule of Life:

Practical

- Enables us to make better use of our time

- Provides a vehicle for our prayer life to mature and deepen over time

- Provides a firm structure for our prayer life so that it is regular and balanced

- Remains flexible

Spiritual

- Leads us to acknowledge and practice the presence of God

- Leads us deeper into the liturgical and sacramental life of the Church

- Supernaturalizes our actions

- Provides for a regular examination of conscience

Practical Considerations in Discerning a Rule of Life

Enables us to make better use of our time

You've probably either said this or heard it, "If it's not on the list, it's not going to happen." A Rule of Life will enable us to make better use of our time and eliminate distractions. It will bring order instead of chaos.

Facilitates a deepening and maturation of our prayer life

Your Rule of Life should be re-examined at least once a year. A prayer schedule that challenges us today will seem second nature later in the year and provide room for additional prayers. With God there is no "time," because He created and transcends it.

Provides a consistent and balanced structure for our prayer life

A Rule of Life requires commitment and practice. What we practice regularly becomes a habit. It also assures a balance of prayer, study and participation in the liturgical and sacramental life of the Church.

Remains flexible

Your Rule of Life must provide some flexibility for demands on your vocation that require you to adjust its length or breadth. If you're a parent with a sick child, your duty of caregiving must take precedence over your desire to pray. So this situation may cause you to alter your prayer schedule for that morning or that day. And it should be noted that in this instance, your care giving is more pleasing to God than your private prayer would have been, because, in your vocational duty, you are responding to God's will for that moment. So for that moment, your active duty becomes your prayer.

Spiritual Considerations in Discerning a Rule of Life

Leads us to acknowledge and practice the presence of God

Truly following the desire for holiness will lead us deeper into communion with God (the purpose for which we were created). "A spirituality of communion dictates above all the heart's contemplations of the mystery of the Trinity dwelling in us and whose light we must also be able to see shining on the face of the brothers and sisters around us."[6] Growing in our understanding and practice of the presence of God will help us to grow in faith, hope and charity.

Leads us deeper into the liturgical and sacramental life of the Church

As Catholics, our entire life should be centered in the liturgical and sacramental life of the Church. This is where we receive the most

6   Pope John Paul II, *Novo Millenio Inuente,* No. 43.

grace and join together in genuine community. "The fruit of the sacramental life is both personal and ecclesial. For every one of the faithful on the one hand, this fruit is life for God in Christ Jesus; for the Church, on the other, it is an increase in charity and in her mission of witness."[7]

Supernaturalizes our actions

By living a Rule of Life, we order our actions towards God and for God, and away from ourselves and our selfish desires. "[A] good Rule provides for brief thought of God before every action of any importance, and for the forming of a supernatural intention. Thus each and every one of our actions is explicitly sanctified and becomes an act of love."[8]

Provides for a regular examination of conscience

A regular examination of conscience teaches us about ourselves and expresses our need for God; thus leading us closer to communion with Him. "In this way, then, the knowledge of God and of self cannot but promise the intimate and affectionate union between the soul and God. Our thirst for happiness and for love is quenched only in Him, Who with His love satiates our heart and all its longings, giving us at once both perfection and bliss."[9]

On the following pages you will find two charts to help you discern your own Rule of Life. After the charts you will find prayers, examens, and devotions to use along the way. Let Our Lady gently guide you through this process over the next three days. Do not try

7 *Catechism of the Catholic Church*, 1134.
8 Rev. Adolphe Tanquerey, S.S., D.D., *The Spiritual Life*, p. 561.
9 Ibid, p. 477.

everything at once. Just begin slowly and let the Holy Spirit guide you. Remember that God loves a cheerful giver. He doesn't consider the size of the gift, only the size of the heart with which it is given.

SOLT Lay Formation Rule of Life

The purpose of this chart is to help you list your current practices (write them in 1 & 2) while discerning your Rule of Life (which you will complete on the following page). BASICS are what you should consider trying to do now. EXTRAS are elements to consider at a later time, after the BASICS are well established.

DAILY Basics

1.

2.

3. Two greatest commandments

4. Morning Offering

5. Rosary

6. Prayer and Examination of Conscience in the evening

DAILY Extras: Daily Mass when possible/Liturgical Readings of the day/Magnificat Prayer, Readings and Meditation/The Divine Office/The Chaplet of Divine Mercy

WEEKLY Basics

1.

2.

3. Participate in the Holy Sacrifice of the Mass on Sunday and Holy Days of Obligation

4. Keep the Lord's Day Holy

5. Family or Community Prayer

WEEKLY Extras: Prepare Readings for the following Sunday/ Thorough Examination of Conscience/Sacrament of Peace and Reconciliation/Honor Mary on Saturday/Participate in Holy Mass at least one weekday/Spend time before Jesus in the Blessed Sacrament/ Holy Hour

MONTHLY Basics

1.

2.

3. Thorough Examination of Conscience

4. Sacrament of Penance and Reconciliation

5. First Friday and First Saturday Mass and Devotion (see pages 207 and 208)

MONTHLY Extras: Time Before Jesus in the Blessed Sacrament/ Complete spiritual reading/Serve those in need/Study an area of faith that interests you

YEARLY Basics

1.

2.

3. Spend two days in silence reflecting on God and your life.

4. Review your Rule of Life and make any necessary changes.

YEARLY Extras: Attend a Directed Retreat/Attend a Catholic Conference on the Faith/Lent: Pray Stations of the Cross on Fridays/

Renew your Consecration to Jesus in Mary

ALWAYS

ALWAYS practice the presence of God. ALWAYS unite any suffering with Christ crucified. ALWAYS make simple acts of self-denial. ALWAYS live Total Consecration. ALWAYS do everything for the love of God. Do you have any ALWAYS Basics that you would like to add to this list?

SOLT Lay Formation Rule of Life

The purpose of the chart on the following page is to help you draft your own Rule of Life. You may wish to consider a visit to Jesus in the Blessed Sacrament as you discern His call for your prayer life. Start simply. It is important to be realistic so that you can be faithful to your Rule.

DAILY Basics: DAILY Extras:

WEEKLY Basics: WEEKLY Extras:

MONTHLY Basics: MONTHLY Extras:

YEARLY Basics: YEARLY Extras:

ALWAYS:

Call to Holiness – Rule of Life

Two Greatest Commandments

You shall love the Lord your God with all your heart, soul, strength and mind, and love your neighbor as yourself.

Morning Offering

"O Jesus, in union with your most Precious Blood that was poured out on the Cross once and offered today at every Mass, I offer you today my prayers, works, joys, sorrows, and suffering for the praise of your Holy Name, and all the desires of your Sacred Heart, the Immaculate Heart of Mary and the Just Heart of Joseph, in reparation for sin, for the conversion of sinners, the union of all Christians, and our final union with you in heaven."

Daily Examination of Conscience

Enter into the presence of God, thanking Him for the gift of your life and the many blessings of your day.

Ask Our Blessed Mother and your Guardian Angel to help you examine your conscience. Pray to the Lord, "Speak, Lord, your servant is listening." Be attentive to the Holy Spirit as you honestly consider the various parts of your day. Examine your conscience.

Imitate Mary

Did I act knowing God is my Father? Was I patient? Was I humble? Was I charitable and not critical of others? Did I keep my attention on materials that would please God? Did I dress modestly? Was I faithful to my prayer life? Was I moderate in my eating and drinking?

Become Like Jesus

Did I give myself willingly and without reserve to all that God asked of me today? Did I unite moments of suffering in love to Christ crucified, acknowledging that they gain merit for me and others? Did I avoid any opportunities to serve others? Was I meek and humble of heart? Was I generous with my time, talent, and treasure? Did I work diligently with the time God gave me?

Live for the Triune God

Did I break any of God's Commandments? Did I purposefully injure my relationship with God, with others, or between others? Did I please God in every thought, word and action? Did I seek to do God's holy will? Did I seek the grace and friendship of God for myself and all others?

Reconciliation

Pray an Act of Contrition with sorrow for any sins committed. *O my God, I am heartily sorry for having offended Thee, and I detest all my sins because of Thy just punishments, but most of all because they offend Thee, my God, Who art all Good and deserving of all my love. I firmly resolve, with the help of Thy grace, to sin no more and to avoid the near occasions of sin.*

Make a firm purpose of amendment and resolve to avoid certain temptations, and to practice a particular virtue.

Confidently ask Jesus, Mary and Joseph to help you. Then pray the Lord's Prayer with them. *Our Father who art in heaven, hallowed be Thy Name. Thy Kingdom come. Thy will be done, on earth as it is in heaven. Give us this day our daily bread, and forgive us our trespasses, as we forgive those who trespass against us, and lead us not into temptation, but deliver us from evil. Amen.*

Daily Mass

Check your parish bulletin and/or diocesan website for the daily Mass times in your area. If possible, participate in one or more daily Masses each week.

"He who receives Communion is made holy and Divinized in soul and body in the same way that water, set over a fire, becomes boiling.... Communion works like yeast that has been mixed into dough so that it leavens the whole mass; .... Just as by melting two candles together you get one piece of wax, so, I think, one who receives the Flesh and Blood of Jesus is fused together with Him by this Communion, and the soul finds that he is in Christ and Christ is in him" (St. Cyril of Alexandria).

"God in his omnipotence could not give more, in His wisdom He knew not how to give more, in His riches He had not more to give, than the Eucharist" (St. Augustine).

Readings of the Day

To find the readings of the day, look in your parish bulletin or parish website. Or you can purchase a Weekday Missal and a Sunday Missal, or go to the United States Conference of Catholic Bishops' website, www.usccb.org (Click on the "Readings" tab at the top of the homepage.)

Magnificat

The *Magnificat* is an exceptional monthly publication that provides the daily readings, morning and evening prayers, articles on saints and daily meditations. There is also a children's version for the Sunday liturgy: *MagnifiKid*. The *Magnificat* website is www.magnificat.com.

The Divine Office

Reciting the Divine Office is a beautiful way to live the liturgical year of the Church and unite your prayers with the universal Church. It provides prayers to be said throughout the day. Volumes are available at Catholic bookstores locally and online.

The *Catechism of the Catholic Church* states that:

> **1174** The mystery of Christ, his Incarnation and Passover, which we celebrate in the Eucharist especially at the Sunday assembly, permeates and transfigures the time of each day through the celebration of the **Liturgy of the Hours**, "the divine office." (Cf. *Sacrosanctum concilium* [SC], ch. IV, 83-101) This celebration, faithful to the apostolic exhortations to "pray constantly," is "so devised that the whole course of the day and night is made holy by the praise of God." (SC 84; 1 Thess 5:17; Eph 6:18) In this "public prayer of the Church," (SC 98) the faithful (clergy, religious, and lay people) exercise the royal priesthood of the baptized. Celebrated in "the form approved" by the Church, the **Liturgy of the Hours** "is truly the voice of the Bride herself, addressed to her Bridegroom. It is the very prayer which Christ himself together with his Body, addresses to the Father." (SC 84) [emphasis added]

Chaplet of Divine Mercy

How to Recite the Chaplet of Divine Mercy

The Chaplet of Divine Mercy is recited with an ordinary Rosary. At the National Shrine of Divine Mercy in Stockbridge, Massachusetts, the Chaplet is preceded by two opening prayers from the Diary of Saint Faustina, and followed by a closing prayer (www.thedivinemercy.org/message/devotions/praythechaplet.php).

Three O'clock Hour of Mercy Prayers (optional)

You expired, Jesus, but the source of life gushed forth for souls, and the ocean of mercy opened up for the whole world. O Fount of Life, unfathomable Divine Mercy, envelop the whole world and empty Yourself out upon us. (Jesus asks that we place ourselves in His abandonment at the moment of agony, even if we can only do this for a brief moment.)

O Blood and Water, which gushed forth from the Heart of Jesus as a fountain of Mercy for us, I trust in You!

Begin with the Our Father, the Hail Mary and the Apostle's Creed:

Our Father

Our Father who art in heaven, hallowed be Thy Name. Thy Kingdom come. Thy will be done, on earth as it is in heaven. Give us this day our daily bread, and forgive us our trespasses, as we forgive those who trespass against us, and lead us not into temptation, but deliver us from evil. Amen.

Hail Mary

Hail Mary, Full of Grace, the Lord is with thee. Blessed art thou among women, and blessed is the fruit of thy womb, Jesus. Holy Mary, Mother of God, pray for us sinners now, and at the hour of death. Amen.

The Apostle's Creed

I believe in God, the Father almighty, creator of heaven and earth. I believe in Jesus Christ, his only Son, Our Lord. He was conceived by the power of the Holy Spirit and born of the Virgin Mary. He suffered under Pontius Pilate, was crucified, died, and was buried. He descended into hell. On the third day he arose again. He ascended into heaven and is seated at the right hand of the Father. He will come again to judge the living and the dead. I believe in the Holy Spirit, the holy catholic Church, the communion of saints, the forgiveness of sins, the resurrection of the body, and the life everlasting. Amen.

Then, on the large bead before each decade

Eternal Father, I offer you the Body and Blood, Soul and Divinity of Your Dearly Beloved Son, Our Lord Jesus Christ, in atonement for our sins and those of the whole world.

On the ten small beads of each decade, say

For the sake of His sorrowful Passion, have mercy on us and on the whole world.

Conclude with (Say 3 Times)

Holy God, Holy Mighty One, Holy Immortal One, have mercy on us and on the whole world.

Optional Closing Prayer

Eternal God, in whom mercy is endless and the treasury of

compassion inexhaustible, look kindly upon us and increase Your mercy in us, that in difficult moments we might not despair nor become despondent, but with great confidence submit ourselves to Your holy will, which is Love and Mercy itself.

Our Lord said to Saint Faustina, "Encourage souls to say the Chaplet which I have given you. … Whoever will recite it will receive great mercy at the hour of death. … When they say this chaplet in the presence of the dying, I will stand between my Father and the dying person, not as the Just Judge but as the Merciful Savior. … Priests will recommend it to sinners as their last hope of salvation. Even if there were a sinner most hardened, if he were to recite this chaplet only once, he would receive grace from my infinite mercy. I desire to grant unimaginable graces to those souls who trust in My mercy. … Through the Chaplet you will obtain everything, if what you ask for is compatible with My will."

Keep the Sabbath Day Holy

Make every effort to keep Sundays holy. John Paul II offered us some beautiful direction in his Apostolic Letter *Dies Domini*:

> "The Lord's Day—as Sunday was called from Apostolic times—has always been accorded special attention in the history of the Church because of its close connection with the very core of the Christian mystery.
>
> "The duty to keep Sunday holy, especially by sharing in the Eucharist and by relaxing in a spirit of Christian joy and fraternity, is easily understood if we consider the many

different aspects of this day upon which the present Letter will focus our attention.

"Sunday is a day which is at the very heart of the Christian life. From the beginning of my Pontificate, I have not ceased to repeat: 'Do not be afraid! Open, open wide the doors to Christ!' In the same way, today I would strongly urge everyone to rediscover Sunday: Do not be afraid to give your time to Christ!"

You can read the entire text at: www.usccb.org/comm/archives/diesdomini.shtml

Family or Community Prayer

If you are not already part of a prayer community, discern a group or form a group for weekly prayer. At these weekly gatherings, you can recite the Rosary, adore Jesus in the Blessed Sacrament, review the Sunday readings, or enjoy another type of prayer or devotion. Of course, families should pray the daily Rosary together. Families that pray together stay together!

Readings for the Following Sunday

Given that the family should try to live the teachings and grace contained in the liturgy throughout the week, sometime in the week you should review the readings for the upcoming Sunday. Begin to integrate those teachings into your life, this week, as you prepare to participate in the liturgy of the Word in the Holy Sacrifice of the Mass. Repeat this process each week.

Sacrament of Penance and Reconciliation

Try to receive the Sacrament of Penance and Reconciliation at least once a month (once every week is better). You will notice a significant difference in your heart and soul. Prior to going, make a thorough examination of conscience and utilize the following guidelines for a good Confession. Before beginning these steps, pray to the Holy Spirit for His light and His grace.

1) Make an **examination of conscience**. You may review the Ten Commandments or go through the beatitudes and pray about how well you're living them. Consider whether or not you have been pleasing to God in every thought, word and action. Have you loved as Jesus has instructed us to love?

2) **Be sorry for your sins** and try to have the perfect sorrow of love (perfect contrition). Remember, Jesus becomes so "small" in the Eucharist for us, and we offend Him. Say, "I am sorry, Lord. You came all the way from heaven and died on the Cross for me; You rose and gave me life. I am sorry. Lord Jesus Christ, have mercy on me, a sinner."

3) **Make a firm resolution not to sin again** and to avoid the near occasion of sin. Ask for this grace through Our Lady.

4) Tell all your sins in the confessional and receive absolution. **Hide nothing**—give it all to God. Remember, serious sins must be confessed by type and number. Clear all the channels of grace.

5) **Say your penance promptly.**

Obtaining a Plenary Indulgence

• Fulfill the indulgenced act (praying the Holy Rosary in church, praying the Way of the Cross, praying at least a half hour in Eucharistic Adoration, reading Scripture or spiritual writings for at least one-half hour, or making other acts that receive a plenary indulgence as declared by the Sacred Penitentiary).

- Go to the Sacrament of Penance and Reconciliation (Confession) within eight days before or eight days after the indulgenced act. (Going to Confession every two weeks automatically fulfills this). It is imperative to go to Confession before receiving Holy Communion if you are conscious of a grave sin.

- Receive Holy Communion in a state of grace on the day of the indulgenced act.

- Pray for the Holy Father's intentions on the day of the indulgenced act. (One Our Father and one Hail Mary said for the Holy Father's intentions will suffice.)

- Be free from all attachment to sin, even venial sin.

Try to gain many plenary indulgences by incorporating them into your Rule of Life. You can work toward gaining an indulgence every day. Don't worry about who to offer them for because you can give them to Our Lady, who applies them in the best possible way.

Honor Mary Especially on Saturdays

Meditate on the gift of Our Blessed Mother and her loving concern and intercession for us. Pray the Rosary and the Angelus and discern good spiritual reading about her life (*Meet Mary* by Dr. Mark Miravalle is available at www.ewtnreligiouscatalogue.com).

Spend Time Before the Blessed Sacrament

Pope Benedict XVI says "how beneficial the rediscovery of Eucharistic adoration by many Christians is…. How much need modern humanity has to rediscover the source of its hope in the Sacrament of the Eucharist! I thank the Lord because many parishes, alongside the devout celebration of Mass, are educating the faithful in Eucharistic adoration. And it is my hope that—also in view of the next International Eucharistic Congress—this practice will become ever more widespread" (Pope Benedict XVI, Vatican City, Nov. 9 2006).

Jesus is waiting for you in the Most Blessed Sacrament, residing in the tabernacle in your Catholic Church. And in some parishes, He is exposed in a monstrance in Perpetual Adoration. Go and visit Him. He is there for you!

Spiritual Reading

Spiritual reading is so underestimated, yet so important. We should always be reading at least one spiritual book at any given time. Maybe you're interested in the saints, or a particular saint. Or maybe you're fascinated by Eucharistic Miracles or the Early Church. You can find good books from Catholic publishers at Emmaus Road Publishing, Sophia Press, Scepter Publishers, Ascension Press, Our Sunday Visitor or Ignatius Press. You can visit a parish library, or you can simply read the Bible.

Serve in the Holy Mass

Serving in the Holy Sacrifice of the Mass is a gift from God. You are blessed as you learn more about the Mass and serve the people in your parish. All the faithful are called to have full, active and conscious participation in the Holy Sacrifice of the Mass. Arrive at the Church early and pray and prepare to enter the central Mystery of our life.

Study an Area of Particular Interest of the Faith

What do you want to learn more about? The Vatican website (www.vatican.va) is an incredible source for information on today's most important issues. EWTN's website (www.ewtn.com) and New Advent's website (www.newadvent.org) similarly have extensive resource libraries. Also, our website (www.OurLadyLovesYou.org) has more fully developed teachings for *Fiat!* and has an extensive resource section.

Practice the Presence of God

Live each day remembering that God created you, that He loves you, and that He has a plan for you.

- Seek the direction of the Holy Spirit in all of your affairs and frequently pray, "Jesus, I Trust in You."

- Look upon God in His goodness and greatness and upon yourself as His child.*

- Keep in mind (attentively and humbly) the many examples of God's love that you have received at His hands, and the treasures of grace that He has showered upon you.*

- Praise the greatness of the Triune God and praise His divine

* Fr. James Flanagan, *SOLT Rules of the Spiritual Life of the Society of Our Lady of the Most Holy Trinity*, p. 70, Rule No. 260.

Majesty for all the blessings and works evident to the eyes of
your soul.*

Unite All Suffering with Christ Crucified

- All suffering should be looked upon as a blessing.*

- Unite all suffering with Christ to fill up what is wanting in the
  sufferings of Christ.*

- Welcome trials, sorrows, and labors with tranquility of soul,
  patience, and lively faith, trusting in the goodness of your
  heavenly Father.*

- Remember that Our Lady stood with Jesus at the Cross, and that
  she will always stand with you, interceding for you during times
  of suffering.

Make Simple Acts of Self Denial

- Be conscious of how blessed you are by God with food, clothing
  and shelter. Make sacrifices to unite yourself with your brothers
  and sisters around the world who have much less.

- Know that prayerfully fasting from food, drink and comforts in a
  balanced way greatly strengthens your spirit.

True Devotion

- After having made your Total Consecration to Jesus through
  Mary, faithfully prepare and renew your consecration each year
  on the same feast day. Each year you will gain insight and grow

in your love for Jesus and Mary.

• Live Total Consecration to Jesus through Mary.

Chapter Six

"How do I live a life of virtue?"

People are asking, "How do I live a life of virtue?" The answer is: "Jesus." Let us begin now by praying the "Our Father" along with Jesus, the All-Virtuous One:

In the name of the Father and of the Son and of the Holy Spirit. Amen.

Our Father who art in heaven, hallowed be Thy Name. Thy Kingdom come. Thy will be done, on earth as it is in heaven. Give us this day our daily bread, and forgive us our trespasses, as we forgive those who trespass against us, and lead us not into temptation, but deliver us from evil. Amen.

Our Lady of the Most Holy Trinity, pray for us.

In the name of the Father and of the Son and of the Holy Spirit. Amen.

Then God said: "Let us make man in our image, after our likeness. Let them have dominion over the fish of the sea, birds of the air, and the cattle, and over all the wild animals and all the creatures that crawl on the ground" (Genesis 1:26).

As you are progressing through this process of formation, remember to thank God Our Father for drawing you into a deeper relationship with Him. One of the principal goals of formation is to know God as Our Father. We need to grow into complete trust of Our Father's goodness and always be able to cry out, "Abba, Father, Daddy!" Our Lady has been sharing with you her relationship with God the Father. Our Father wants you to be happy, so He wants you to live a life of Holiness and Virtue. Virtue is the heart of the third part of the *Catechism* which begins by quoting St. Leo the Great:

> "Christian, recognize your dignity and, now that you share in God's own nature, do not return to your former base condition by sinning. Remember who is your head and of whose body you are a member. Never forget that you have been rescued from the power of darkness and brought into the light of the kingdom of God."

This reminds us of everything that we have learned so far. We have come to understand that God has a plan and purpose for us. We have prayed and we continue to pray for guidance and grace to become holy, happy, and to reach heaven. We have come to understand that we are created in the image and likeness of God—we know our dignity. "Christian, recognize your dignity."

What is virtue, anyway? Here's a good definition from the *Catechism:*

> **1803** A virtue is an habitual and firm disposition to do the good. It allows the person not only to perform good acts, but to give the best of himself. The virtuous person tends

toward the good with all his sensory and spiritual powers; he pursues the good and chooses it in concrete actions.

What a beautiful way of life! In the Book of Micah we hear, *He has showed you, O man, what is good; and what does the LORD require of you but to do justice, and to love kindness, and to walk humbly with your God... (Micah 6:8).* Our Lady fulfills this call of Sacred Scripture. Virtue is relevant to our lives. The virtuous person is a happy person and brings happiness everywhere he or she goes, and strives for virtue regardless of the situation. St. Louis Marie de Montfort teaches us that Our Lady has ten principal virtues that we must imitate. Anyone would be very happy to possess all ten of these virtues in abundance. So they are listed below for you to consider. We will then review each one more fully.

10 Principal Virtues of Our Lady (St. Louis de Montfort)

- Profound Humility

- Lively Faith

- Blind Obedience (Unswerving Allegiance to Jesus and His Church)

- Continual Mental Prayer

- Mortification in All Things

- Surpassing Purity

- Ardent Charity

- Heroic Patience

- Angelic Sweetness

- Divine Wisdom

Our Lady is the perfect model of virtue. When we think of virtuous people, we think of the saints, of whom Mary is the Queen. The Holy Father, Pope Benedict XVI, wrote, "Knowing a little

about the history of saints and understanding that in the causes of
canonization there is inquiry into 'heroic' virtue, we almost inevitably
have a mistaken concept of holiness: 'It is not for me,' we are led to
think, 'because I do not feel capable of attaining heroic virtue. It is too
high a goal.' Holiness then becomes a thing reserved for some 'greats'
whose images we see on the altars, and who are completely different
from us ordinary sinners. But this is a mistaken notion of holiness."[10]

Have you felt that way? Maybe while glancing through stories of
the saints or looking upon stained glass windows? Do you think about
the saints and say, "That's too hard for me," or "That was then, but this
is now"?

Heroic virtue is *not* doing great and very visible things on our
own. Heroic virtue is the abandonment of self at each moment,
remaining open and energetic to do God's will. Heroic virtue is to be
present and available for God to work in and through us. Again, the
Holy Father reminds us, "Christian sacrifice consists in our becoming
totally receptive and letting ourselves be completely taken over by
God—letting Him act on us."[11]

Recall the words of Jesus in the Gospel of Matthew and hear them
spoken to you:

> *"You, therefore, must be perfect, as your heavenly Father
> is perfect."*[12]

- -

10 Joseph Cardinal Ratzinger, "Letting God Work," *L'Osservatore Romano*,
   October 6, 2002.
11 Pope Benedict XVI, Introduction for Friday of the 15th Week of Ordinary Time,
   Magnificat, July 17, 2009, pg. 249.
12 Matthew 5:46.

Your Father in heaven, who created you, is calling you to live heroic virtue and holiness.

The *Catechism of the Catholic Church* teaches us that "'All Christians in any state or walk of life are called to the fullness of Christian life and to the perfection of charity' (LG 40 S 2). All are called to holiness."[13]

All of us are called to live the life of Christ—a life of virtue and holiness. If you live a life of prayer and you are open to the power of the Holy Spirit, allowing yourself to be transformed by the Lord from glory to glory, then you will learn to *Imitate Mary, Become Like Jesus and Live for the Triune God*. You will be living a life of virtue—the life of holiness. Within this life of virtue and holiness, you will find true love, deep peace, and everlasting joy. Are you ready to give it a try?

DAY ONE – Imitating Mary in Virtue

As a human person, Our Blessed Mother responded perfectly to the will of God and lived a virtuous life as the first and perfect disciple of Jesus. We too are disciples of Jesus, and Jesus gives us His Blessed Mother as both an advocate and a perfect model to emulate in following Him. So let us turn to Our Lady's life, the foundation of this formation program. There is a relational reality in this formation program. It is not just about book knowledge. Book knowledge is good, but relationships are superior, for relationships are what we are created for. Our relationships will be blessed through a life of virtue. So let us now examine the ten principal virtues of the Blessed Virgin

---

13 *Catechism of the Catholic Church*, 2013.

Mary. After reading through the list, please choose just one virtue at a time to pray about and consider more fully.

Profound Humility

Our Lady lived in profound humility. She recognized that she was created out of nothing from God's goodness. She kept her vision (her heart) on the greatness of God. She viewed everything that she received as a gift. She considered herself lowly, yet God bestowed on her His greatest gift— Jesus Christ. The Holy Spirit came upon Our Blessed Mother when she said "yes" to the plan of God. Jesus, seeing her profound humility, descended from heaven, *and the Word became flesh and dwelt among us*. Humility moves God. Do you want to please God? God cannot resist humility. We see the humility of Christ that Our Blessed Mother embraces—humility pleases God. According to St. Augustine, humility is the foundation of all virtue. Humility is the foundation of a life of virtue and a life of God. Therefore, embrace humility, learn from Our Lady, and pray to be humble. Ask Our Lady to teach you about her Son Jesus, who is meek and humble of heart.

Lively Faith

Our Lady moved in lively faith. Faith and humility go together because faith teaches us who God is. And when you truly understand who God is (when you know His greatness—that He fills the whole universe and is the Creator of all) then you will bow down humbly before Our Lord and Maker, Our King and Our God. When you have lively faith, you will be humble. Humility is keeping our littleness connected with God's greatness. And when faith and humility come together, God

works wonders in the humble heart. Faith is one of three theological
virtues, given so that we can relate to God and live a supernatural life.
Our Lady exemplified Faith by saying "Yes!" to God's plan. In saying
"Yes," Mary is the first human person to have a glimpse of the Holy
Trinity revealed to her. This little 15 year old girl (holy and pure, full
of love and grace) said "Yes!" to God's plan, even though she knew it
was humanly impossible. She said "Yes!" and we are to say "Yes!" We
walk by faith and not by sight. Faith precedes understanding. We don't
say, "Prove it to me before I'll believe it." That's arrogant and proud.
We are finite. God is infinite. God came from heaven to reveal His
infinite love for us and to reveal who He is. Live a life of faith. Pray for
that gift of faith—it is a gift.

Blind Obedience

The third principal virtue of Our Blessed Mother is blind obedience.
Or said in a way that might resonate more clearly in modern times:
"unswerving allegiance to Jesus and His Church." Our Lady didn't
just close her eyes and walk into walls—far from it. Blind obedience
means that she was blind to herself. Her vision was fixed on God
and God alone. Remember her words to the Angel Gabriel, when he
informed her of God's plan for her life: *"Behold, I am the handmaid
of the Lord. May it be done to me according to your word" (Luke
1:38).* Remember also her words to the servers at the wedding at
Cana: *"Do whatever he tells you" (John 2:5).* Mary intimately knew
that God has our best interests at heart, and she lived her life in
obedient accordance. Similarly, Jesus, the God-man, encourages us to
holy obedience, promising us complete fulfillment if we stay faithful

to him: *"If you remain in my word, you will truly be my disciples, and you will know the truth, and the truth will set you free"* (Jn. 8:31-32). Jesus communicates His teachings, His truth, through His Catholic Church, which Scripture describes as *"the pillar and foundation of truth"* (1 Timothy 3:15). Indeed, Jesus speaks to us through His Church and not simply through Scripture, as Scripture affirms that Jesus commissioned His apostles and their successors to advance His Kingdom: *"Go, therefore, and make disciples of all nations, baptizing them in the name of the Father, and of the Son, and of the Holy Spirit, teaching them to observe all that I have commanded you"* (Matthew 28:19-20).

The Church's God-given authority applies not only to Our Lord's teaching but also to guiding His people in matters of governance and discipline, as Jesus conveyed to Peter, the first Pope: *"I will give you the keys to the kingdom of heaven. Whatever you bind on earth shall be bound in heaven; and whatever you loose on earth shall be loosed in heaven"* (Matthew 16:19. cf. 18:15-18). So obedience to Christ extends to obedience to the teachings and lawful actions of His Church, which serves in His name. (The term "lawful actions" would necessarily exclude unlawful, immoral actions like clerical sexual abuse, which gravely deviate from the mission of Christ and His Church.)

And our obedience should not be motivated by fear, but rather great charity and gratitude for what Our Lord has done in giving Himself completely on our behalf. Jesus both models this love and exhorts us to love Him and others by emulating Him: *"This is my commandment: love one another as I love you "* (John 15:12).

Today, many people scoff at obedience. They set themselves up as the sole authority in everything, and that is terrifying. When some hear about blind obedience for the first time, they think, "I don't know if I can do this. What does it mean? Am I not supposed to think?" No! It means that you're supposed to think *even more*—about God, about who you are, about your destiny, about love, about happiness. That's what blind obedience means. Do not be deceived by the devil or the world. Learn to love authentically We know that selfish people cannot love. Selfish people can only "love" themselves. They are not able to love the way they're supposed to love. However, people who have blind obedience or unswerving allegiance to Jesus and His Church—like Our Blessed Mother and the saints—are able to love authentically. As Jesus says, *"The truth sets them free."* They become extraordinarily happy, always peaceful, and always content. Follow this call to virtue. Pray for the blessed virtue of blind obedience.

Continual Mental Prayer

Our Blessed Mother lived in continual mental prayer. Our Lady prays always. Some people think that if they always pray they won't be able to work (sanctifying their home and workplace), which is what the lay faithful are supposed to do. Remember, however, that when you make a morning offering and cover yourself with the virtues and merits of Jesus, Mary and Joseph, your whole day becomes a prayer. When you learn to live like Our Lady, you learn how to move like her. In Christ, we live and move and have our being. So if you stay in the hearts of Jesus, Mary and Joseph (by doing the Father's will in all things) you can be praying and serving all the time.

The Benedictines have a little motto, *Ora et Labora*—prayer
and work. Prayer is the work of the soul and work is the prayer of
the body. You see, our whole life is integrated. The problem with
society today is that we're not integrated—we're disintegrated and we
disintegrate. There is a grave lack of virtue in today's world. The world
needs an infusion of virtue. We pray for this infusion of virtue. But
how is it going to happen? It begins with you. It begins with humility
by turning to God. We learn from Our Lady—profound humility, lively
faith, blind obedience and continual mental prayer. Pray for the virtue
of continual mental prayer.

Mortification

Our Blessed Mother lived a life of mortification in all things. Most
people don't understand mortification, and sometimes people recoil at
the thought of self-denial. But in reality, mortification is the necessary
path to our freedom, for it frees us of self. Mortification comes from
the Latin root *morte*, which means "to die." We are to die to ourselves
in order to rise in Christ to a higher way of life—a Divine Way of
life—a virtuous way of life. This flows from our communion with
God. Mortification in all things really means that we are not possessed
by our possessions. Many people are possessed by possessions. They
say, "I must have this, and I need the latest of that." There is blessing
in everything when you keep your vision on God, for the blessing is
not in the thing itself, but in Our Father who gives it. Mortification in
all things frees us from selfishness and sin. With mortification, we are
bound to God in our spirit, rather than bound to things in our flesh.
We become liberated from the slavery of the flesh.

Too many people have given in to the sins of the flesh, and they have become slaves. We don't want to be slaves. Virtue sets us free. Vice (which is the opposite of virtue) imprisons you. Virtue is doing the good. Vice is when people fall into the bad. We want good habits, so we need to be disciplined. The word "discipline" relates to the word "disciple". Disciples are disciplined. People that are disciplined are free. Blind obedience to Christ and His Church, as well as mortification in all things, sets us free. Because when we die to ourself, we rise in Christ. Too many people have fallen into vice (alcohol, drugs, pornography) and they become slaves to it. We all know people that are enslaved. We must pray for them to break free in Christ. Our Lady will take them by the hand and help them if they desire it. Is there an area of your life that needs mortification? You might think that there is no help for you. Maybe you just began this program. You might think that it was just by chance, but nothing is by chance. Everything is in God's providence. God loves you and He wants you to be free. He doesn't want you to be trapped in a bottle. He doesn't want you to be trapped in impurity, or enslaved to vice. God will set you free if you respond to His call.

Come to Our Blessed Mother as your mother, and she will help you. Mortification in all things is the way. Let us be free from vice and follow our call to the virtuous way of life. Praise God for giving us the Blessed Virgin Mary and her model of virtue. Mortification in all things is such a blessing. Let us continually pray for this virtue.

Surpassing Purity

Our Blessed Mother lived a life of surpassing purity. Most people only address purity of the flesh because they are failing to live purity at that level. The highest level of purity is to love God with all your heart, soul, strength and mind. In living at this highest level of purity, your life will be abundantly blessed. That is the surpassing purity of the Blessed Mother—she kept her vision fixed on God. When you love God with all your heart, soul, strength and mind, everything else takes care of itself. Many people are stuck in the battle of the flesh and they are losing ground, because we are not created for the flesh. In the area of the flesh, it is appropriate that we deny ourselves; but let us not lose our focus on God. Everything we have belongs to God, so let us keep our vision fixed on Him.

Regarding the life of an ordained priest of the New and Everlasting Covenant, thank God that we have a vow or promise of celibacy. The celibate life allows us to be mystically espoused to the Church, the bride of Christ, in general, rather than to one woman in sacramental marriage. The wonderful, two-in-one-flesh communion of husband and wife, and the procreation and education of children that accompanies it, is unique to the vocation of marriage. Yet, priestly fathers are also wonderfully fruitful but in a different way—by serving the intimate spiritual needs of many people. So the celibate priesthood is a great gift. Similarly conjugal love, and the two-in-one-flesh communion of husband and wife in general, are also great gifts, and they're reserved for the sanctity of Holy Matrimony. That is how God arranged it—something sacred. You are a temple of God. You are sacred. So conduct yourself in a holy and virtuous way.

The best way to grow in purity is to stay close to Our Lady and look to her life. Study the fullness of her life in the four dogmas of the faith taught by the Church on Our Blessed Mother: her Immaculate Conception, her Perpetual Virginity, her Motherhood of God, and her Assumption (body and soul into heaven). Ask Our Lady to pray with you for the virtue of surpassing purity.

Ardent Charity

Our Blessed Mother lived a life of ardent charity. She is ardent with great zeal and fervor. Remember the words that St. Paul says in Sacred Scripture, *So faith, hope, love abide, these three; but the greatest of these is love (I Corinthians 13:13).* Faith, hope and charity (or love) are what we call "Theological Virtues." We cannot give them to ourselves. They can only be given to us by God. God Himself is charity. We are creatures (just like Our Lady); but when we relate to God, who is uncreated Charity, and when we have a proper relationship with Him, charity is manifested in our life. That is the only way that we can have charity. The definition of the theological virtue of charity is to love God above all things for his own sake, and our neighbor as ourselves out of love for God. Everyone who is sent into our lives, and everything that happens in our lives takes place under the loving care of Our Father. Certainly, there is evil in the world. God permits it for now, but He always draws good out of everything for those who love Him (cf. Romans 8:28).

Loving God with all your heart, soul, strength and mind will flow from the virtue of ardent charity. Charity enables us to see the goodness of the Father in everyone and everything, and from that charity love for others will flow. Love is fundamentally the disposition to please the Beloved who is God the Father. If you spend your life pleasing Our Father in everything you do, you will be living the life of Jesus and Mary. Our Lady will help you. That's virtue. That's joy. That's happiness. That's peace. That's strength.

The word virtue comes from the Latin word *vir* which means "man." It means strength and courage. Men were thought to be full of strength and courage. We pray for true people of God—not selfish but self-giving. The measure of a person is where he lays down his life. The virtuous person can lay down his life for others. It takes strength to lay down your life. Jesus laid down His life "for all men without exception" (*CCC* 605; cf., *CCC* 776, 1260). We are called to lay down our lives. We are called to have a sacrificial love. We are called to have an inspired understanding which energizes heroic leadership. Most people have just one of these three blessings in their life. It is wonderful to experience someone who has all three—sacrificial love, inspired understanding and heroic leadership! These people are an inspiration to us all. We are called to this degree of love, and Our Lady will teach us the way. In order to attain it, we need the virtue of ardent charity—pray for this virtue.

Heroic Patience

The next principal virtue of Our Lady is heroic patience. A great definition of holiness is to live heroic virtue according to your state in life, at all times, and in all places. So sanctity includes four aspects: 1) living heroic virtue, 2) according to your state in life, 3) at all times, and 4) in all places. We are created to be saints. So this is a good definition of how we are supposed to live—with heroic virtue.

It isn't virtue *some* of the time, but *all* of the time, in every situation, according to our state in life. But we know better than to try this on our own. We have to live this heroic patience through, with and in Jesus! Trying to be heroically patient on your own can only lead to disaster. When we're tested in patience, we should thank God for the opportunity to grow in patience. The fruit of the fourth sorrowful mystery (the Carrying of the Cross) is patience. When you get tired of carrying your cross, it's because you're trying to carry it alone. You need to carry it in Jesus. Even Jesus carried His cross in the will of the Father, strengthened by the Holy Spirit, with Our Lady by His side. And Our Lady is there for you, too.

So the next time you get frustrated while standing in the check-out line or while caught in traffic, recognize it as a gift. Turn to Our Lady and pray a Hail Mary. Our Lady will pray for you now and at the hour of your death. Then pray for the other people around you in the uncomfortable situation. God brings us together in life because we need each other to help one another grow in virtue. We don't say, "Well, *that* one sure is making me grow in virtue!" We pray for everyone to grow in virtue. To do the will of the Father, through, with, and in Jesus, in the power of the Holy Spirit—that is heroic patience. So let us grow in patience by turning to Our Lady. Let us pray for the virtue of heroic patience.

Angelic Sweetness

Our Lady lived a life of angelic sweetness. We are not angels. But we can learn how to be sweet from the angels. It's beautiful to hear people say, "Sweet Jesus, my sweet Savior." They are not talking about candy, but the true sweetness of His pleasing presence. When a man falls in love with a beautiful woman, he calls her "sweetheart". Isn't it wonderful to have a sweetheart—someone who brings sweetness to our life? That's what Our Lady does. She lives a life of angelic sweetness, and she will teach it to us. Let us pray for the virtue of angelic sweetness.

Divine Wisdom

Our Lady was filled with Divine Wisdom. You are reading about her ten principal virtues, but remember that Our Lady is perfect in all the virtues because she is the Spouse of the Holy Spirit. The Holy Spirit perfects His virtues and His gifts in us. That's how it works.

Our Lady is filled with divine wisdom, and that is exactly what this world needs. Worldly wisdom does not offer long-term solutions. For lifelong guidance and direction, we need a wisdom that comes from above. We encounter so many challenges that we need divine wisdom. God is asking you to give yourself to Him, that in Him and through Him you can enter into His plan for the salvation of the world. God is asking you to become part of the solution to the current world problems. And the solution that the world needs today is through divine wisdom—not human wisdom.

It is a gift to be educated, to apply our knowledge, and to act in a way that is intelligent and reasonable. We need divine solutions to worldly problems, and Our Lady will help us by showing us divine wisdom. She also helps us to keep an eternal perspective on everything, remembering why we are here, where we are from, and where we are going. Pray for the seven Gifts of the Holy Spirit and His fruitfulness in your life—a life of perfection. Our Lady will obtain these gifts for you if you ask her.

These are the ten principal virtues of Our Blessed Mother. We could have approached virtue in many ways, but studying Our Lady's life and imitating her is the sure, short and perfect way to become like Jesus and live for the Triune God.

- Virtue is necessary to live in freedom and peace.

- Virtue is necessary to live the life of Christ, in whom we are baptized.

- Virtue is pleasing to God because it sets us free to love spontaneously. It sets us free to do the will of God and to arrive at our destiny.

- Stay close to Our Lady and imitate her virtues so that you can become a saint.

Take one of these principal virtues and start to work on it because all of the virtues are connected. If you grow in one virtue, all the others will follow. Pick a virtue and start to grow. Be open to this call. The grace of this life is freedom. You are called to live a virtuous life— you are called to be free!

DAY TWO – Becoming Like Jesus in Virtue

Jesus prayed to the Father with His Sacred Heart and lived each moment for the Father's will. In order to become like Jesus and live a virtuous life, you must first learn to pray like Jesus. Listen to the words of Sacred Scripture (Luke 22:39-42):

And he came out, and went, as was his custom, to the

Mount of Olives; and the disciples followed him. And
when he came to the place he said to them, "Pray that
you may not enter into temptation." And he withdrew
from them about a stone's throw, and knelt down and
prayed, "Father, if thou art willing, remove this cup from
me; nevertheless not my will, but thine, be done."

Here in the Garden of Gethsemane, Jesus prepares to face his
Passion and Death. In the Agony of the Garden, we are given the
opportunity to see Christ's virtues which are His way to fulfill the
will of the Father. In spite of His agony, He is teaching us and
showing us the way to holiness—the way of virtue. In particular,
we witness His:

- Humility—He falls to His knees to prepare for a sacrifice (for a
  burden of sin that is not His own).

- Obedience—Understanding the impending persecution and
  torture that He will receive, He still offers His will (united with
  the Father's will) to fulfill the Father's plan of redemption.

- Charity—Thinking of each of us (every soul throughout time),
  He fulfills the Father's plan out of love for us—keeping us in
  His heart.

- Wisdom—He accepts humiliation, nothingness, and death over
  self-defense, power, and self-preservation, to offer humanity (us)
  to the Father.

From St. Louis Marie de Montfort we learn, "wisdom is that
prudence of love that has inspired and animated all of the Savior's

choices, in contrast with the wisdom of the world."[14] We need this divine wisdom each day to help us understand that God asks us to make choices that are in contrast with the wisdom of the world. And God asks us to do His will even when we are tempted—most especially when we are tempted.

Following His Baptism in the Jordan River, the Spirit commands Jesus into the desert where He is tempted by the devil. The desert has great relevance to our own temptations and conversion, "for it is there that Jesus enters into solidarity with sinners."[15]

> *For because He himself has suffered and been tempted,*
> *He is able to help those who are tempted (Hebrews 2:18).*

Jesus chose to do all of this out of love for us. It is out of love for us that Jesus lowered Himself to our human state. He fully understands pain, hunger, loneliness and temptation. We want to become like Him and pray like Him and offer our will to the will of the Father. Each day we have constant opportunities to choose for good—to choose for God. Pope Benedict XVI tells us, "At the heart of all temptations, as we see here, is the act of pushing God aside because we perceive him as secondary, if not actually superfluous and annoying, in comparison with all the apparently far more urgent matters that fill our lives."[16] Have you ever pushed God aside because you wanted something or someone else, and He seemed to be in your way? We all do this to a certain degree. But Jesus can give us the strength we need each day to

14 *Jesus Living in Mary: Handbook of the Spirituality of St. Louis de Montfort*-Virtue, Section IV, No. 2.
15 Pope Benedict XVI, *Jesus of Nazareth*, p. 27.
16 Pope Benedict XVI, *Jesus of Nazareth*, p. 28.

make the choice for good—for God. Quite simply, in our daily choices, "the Way" is the will of the Father.

Does God the Father actually care about my little daily decisions? He certainly does, because He loves you. Does He care if you watch television? He cares about what you're watching and how long you're watching it. Does He care if you drink a soda? He becomes concerned if you drink several of them a day. Does He care if you gossip about other people? Yes, because all people are made in His image and likeness. Does He care if you have a boyfriend or girlfriend? He cares most that the relationship is pure in mind, heart and body. Television, Diet Coke, talking with a friend or having a relationship can all be good. Yet, "All evil and sin comes from pursuing a good in [a disordered] way."[17] In solidarity with Jesus, we must be wary of the Tempter, "the Evil One," who is "the author or instigator" of "all evils, present, past and future" (*CCC* 2854). In contrast, when we pursue a good in a disordered way, we succumb to the devil, even if briefly, and place ourselves and our will above God. We thus sin and thereby damage or even break our communion with God (*CCC* 1855-56). Here is the challenge: to grow in holiness you must practice choosing what is truly good and virtuous in your daily decisions. Then when faced with a larger or more tempting situation, you will be stronger to choose for good—for God.

Let us pray:

Dear Father, Son and Holy Spirit, I want to live a life of virtue. I ask for the prayers of Mary and all the holy angels and saints to

. . . .

17 School of Faith, *Virtue: The Art of Happiness*, 2008.

help me do Your will, Father. Though I cannot do this on my own, I know this is possible through Jesus Christ, living in me through the power of the Holy Spirit. Help me, Abba, to choose for you. Help me to live a life of holiness and virtue. Amen.

DAY THREE – Going Deeper with STMD

Is God calling you deeper? Following are ways to go deeper with Jesus, who calls you to see Him revealed in the Bible (Sacred Scripture), orthodox writings of the saints (faithful witness to Sacred Tradition) and the Catechism (Magisterium's faithful exposition of the Deposit of Faith)—STMD.

Jesus, I know You are the answer to all of my questions. Please reveal yourself to me in Sacred Scripture:

> *And he came out, and went, as was his custom, to the Mount of Olives; and the disciples followed him. And when he came to the place he said to them, "Pray that you may not enter into temptation." And he withdrew from them about a stone's throw, and knelt down and prayed, "Father, if thou art willing, remove this cup from me; nevertheless not my will, but thine, be done"*
> *(Luke 22:39-42).*

> *For because He himself has suffered and been tempted, He is able to help those who are tempted (Hebrews 2:18).*

Feel free to find these passages in your Bible and read them in context. You may even want to read them once silently and then out loud. Spend some time thinking about them, and then take them to prayer. It is always a good idea to memorize verses of Sacred Scripture and make them your own. This is just another way to know Jesus (Who is the Eternal Word) a little better.

Jesus, I know You are the answer to all of my questions. Please reveal yourself to me in the orthodox writings of the saints, which provide a faithful witness to Sacred Tradition.

In essence, St. Augustine made the following comments about virtue:

> Virtue is appropriate ordinate (ordered) love. Not simply loving what one ought to love, but loving most who deserves the most love, and all else with a love suited to its worth.

We pray with St. Augustine, "Order love within me." Virtue is basically ordered love. Our Lady will teach you how to live an ordered love. God first—love God with all your heart, soul, strength and mind, and love your neighbor as yourself for the love of God. This is what virtue is all about.

You might want to know more about the saint who is quoted above. A Weekday Missal is a great place to start when you want to know more about certain saints. And there are many good resources on the internet and in the library about great saints.

Jesus, I know You are the answer to all of my questions. Please reveal yourself to me in the Magisterium's faithful exposition of the Deposit of Faith.

You can turn to the *Catechism of the Catholic Church,* number 1803:

A virtue is a habitual and firm disposition to do the good. It allows the person not only to perform good acts, but to give the best of himself. The virtuous person tends toward the good with all his sensory and spiritual powers; he pursues the good and chooses it in concrete actions.

What a beautiful way of life. In the Book of Micah we hear, *He has showed you, O man, what is good; and what does the LORD require of you but to do justice, and to love kindness, and to walk humbly with your God... (Micah 6:8).* Our Lady fulfills this call of Sacred Scripture. Virtue is relevant to our lives. The virtuous person is a happy person and brings happiness everywhere he or she goes, striving for virtue regardless of the situation.

Part Three of the *Catechism*, Life in Christ, will help you understand even more about the life of virtue.

Use this space to write down any additional thoughts, prayers or epiphanies the Lord has given you during this teaching in your spiritual formation:

Chapter Seven

"How do I live the liturgy?"

Liturgy is Life! People are asking, "How do I live the liturgy?" The answer is: "Jesus." Let us begin now by praying the "Our Father" along with Jesus, from Whom the liturgy flows:

In the name of the Father and of the Son and of the Holy Spirit. Amen.

Our Father who art in heaven, hallowed be Thy Name. Thy Kingdom come. Thy will be done, on earth as it is in heaven. Give us this day our daily bread, and forgive us our trespasses, as we forgive those who trespass against us, and lead us not into temptation, but deliver us from evil. Amen.

Our Lady of the Most Holy Trinity, pray for us.

In the name of the Father and of the Son and of the Holy Spirit. Amen.

Sometimes at Mass, while listening to the readings or the homily we think, "That is just what I have been going through lately," or "I really needed to hear that." Well, that is an example of how "Liturgy is Life!" We can receive (through the power of the Holy Spirit and Our

Lady's intercession) the gift of understanding the liturgy, and how God works in our lives through the liturgy. God announces in the liturgy what He is going to do in our lives. God speaks to us through the weekly and the daily liturgy of the Church. Through daily reading and prayer of the 3-year cycle of readings (which are a gift of the Church to us) you can come to realize that "Liturgy is Life!"

This is about your life, and if you want to know how your life will unfold (how God will work in your life), you need to understand the liturgy. The Church offers the Sacrifice of the Mass in the context of the liturgical seasons. The liturgical year begins with the first Sunday of Advent, as we prepare for the birth of Christ. Liturgy is living. For example, the birth of Christ is not just a reality that happened over 2000 years ago. Certainly it was a historical event, but God is God. He is eternal. He is infinite. He is not bound by time and space. He wants to be born in our lives, our hearts, our souls, our spirits, and in our very being. We are baptized into Christ, and that is why we go through the liturgical year—to enter into the mystery of Christ who reveals us to ourselves.

Liturgical Cycle: Advent and Christmas

We continue with the liturgical cycle, revealing how our life is contained in the weekly liturgy. We have Advent, then we come to the birth of Christ at Christmas. Christmas doesn't come and go in one day. We have an Octave of Christmas. Eight days in which every day is celebrated as Christmas. We reflect on the mystery of the Incarnation and the birth of Christ, and the Child being born for us. God becomes man. What does the meaning of this Child and His birth mean to you?

Each year that mystery unfolds in a new and living way.

Liturgical Cycle: Ordinary Time

Then we come to Ordinary Time. The length of the beginning of this Season is variable, so we celebrate anywhere between four to nine weeks of Ordinary Time before the holy season of Lent. Ordinary Time, however, is not ordinary. Nothing about our life is ordinary. Our life is extraordinary. We do ordinary things with extraordinary love, just like St. Thérèse of Lisieux. Let us become friends with the saints. The saints help us through the liturgical year by helping us to understand the mystery of Christ. The saints lived the liturgy, the mystery of Christ. We make friends with the saints, and when their feast days occur, we join them in prayer. At the end of the liturgical year, the final Sunday of Ordinary Time is the Solemnity of Christ the King. This time is not ordinary because He is our destiny.

Liturgical Cycle: Lent, Holy Week and Easter Triduum

Next in the liturgical cycle is Lent. During the holy season of Lent, we experience some beautiful formation. Prayer, fasting and almsgiving are the way of life as we are led by the Holy Spirit into the desert to accompany Jesus as He shows us the way to victory over temptation and sin. Lent ends at the onset of the most solemn days of the liturgical year, the Easter Triduum, beginning with the evening Mass of the Lord's Supper on Holy Thursday and concluding with evening prayer on Easter Sunday.

Liturgical Cycle: Easter Season

On Easter, Jesus rises and comes forth from the tomb with a smile of

joyful triumph on His face. We contemplate His face as He comes forth
to give us a new life. He gives us a new light that guides our lives—the
light of faith. He makes it possible for us to love with His Love. We
enter into the Octave of Easter when we are given eight days to reflect
on the meaning of Jesus' rising from the dead. Death has no more
power over us. Claim the victory! In fact, we have not simply eight
but *fifty days* of the Easter season to claim that victory! Fifty days!
Most people don't recognize that we have fifty days of Easter. Here
we reflect on the meaning of Christ's Resurrection and are consumed
and transformed in the fire of divine love (in the Holy Spirit). Here we
learn to live in oneness with the risen Christ and to witness His Divine
Love. Fifty days—what a gift!

Forty days after Christ's Resurrection is His Ascension (Ascension
Thursday). By His own power, Jesus ascends to heaven. Prior to the
Ascension, Our Blessed Mother asks Jesus for a blessing. We continue
the Easter Season in the Upper Room with Our Blessed Mother
praying with the Apostles for a new outpouring of the Holy Spirit.
Then Pentecost occurs fifty days after Easter. The Holy Spirit comes
forth upon us all, so we have to learn how to "worship and glorify"
and "call upon" the Holy Spirit (*CCC* 685, 2670; cf. 2671). This is not
just some historical event of 2,000 years ago—this is our life. We
must seek a new outpouring of the Holy Spirit each and every day
of our life. We should pray often: *Come, Holy Spirit, come; come by
the means of the powerful intercession of the Immaculate Heart of
Mary, your well-beloved spouse. Come Holy Spirit, renew the face of
the earth. Holy Spirit, you are the soul of the Church, the divine life
of my soul—move me!*

Liturgical Cycle: Trinity Sunday and Corpus Christi

Then we journey into Trinity Sunday. Our community (SOLT) enjoys living its Trinitarian-Marian spirituality. Being members of the Society of Our Lady of the Most Holy Trinity, we live Our Lady's relationships with the Father, the Son and the Holy Spirit. What does it mean to receive the Trinity in our Baptism? How do we live this Trinitarian life? All of this is contained in liturgy.

Then we move to the Feast of Corpus Christi (the Body of Christ, the Eucharist, and the Eucharistic Mystery of Christ). His Passion, Death, Resurrection and Ascension—the Paschal Mystery of Christ— is all contained in the Eucharist. Christ crucified and risen is in the Eucharist. We learn how to live liturgy in the power of the Eucharist. In the Holy Sacrifice of the Mass, the Eucharist empowers us to live the Word proclaimed at the Mass.

Liturgical Cycle: Ordinary Time

Then we move along into another period of Ordinary Time that, again, is not ordinary. Ordinary Time is "ordered time" that brings us into the full mystery of the life of Christ. Proceeding through the liturgical year, we are formed from Sunday to Sunday, hearing how God is going to work in our lives. Each Sunday, God tells us where the graces will be. Each and every Sunday is a compass point in our life. We proceed through the year to the Solemnity of Christ the King, and then we begin the liturgical year again. We have these seasons that proceed through the life of Christ year after year because we are baptized into Christ, and we need to learn to live the mystery of our Baptism. God graces us with liturgical times and seasons, and He forms us in liturgy.

Every part of the Holy Sacrifice of the Mass has deep meaning for us to live. Faith and life are connected.

Liturgy Preparation

The following chart outlines the liturgy in the Mass. Some important definitions follow the chart to increase your understanding of some of the key terms. This chart will be useful as you begin to read ahead in the liturgical schedule to see what God will be doing in your life. Receiving spiritual insights on Sunday is necessary to prepare you for the challenges and formation that will come your way each day throughout the week.

It is particularly important to read ahead for the Sunday liturgy. The Sunday liturgy sets the tone for the entire week. You will notice, through faithful attention to the daily readings, that the lesson taught on Sunday is deepened and developed throughout the week. The Church has given us such a beautiful gift in the 3-year cycle of readings. If you have never considered this gift before, now is the time to do so.

Liturgy preparation is very important because so many precious graces are given to us in the Mass (if we are only prepared to receive them). For grace is received according to the disposition of the receiver. Infinite riches are available to you if you prepare well. When you prepare well, you will be tuned in, your heart will be touched, and you will be enriched. You will be ready for the next week of life as God forms you to *Imitate Mary, Become Like Jesus, and Live for the Triune God.*

LITURGY PREPARATION CHART

Entrance Antiphon	Blessed Trinity, please help me to look at this liturgy from your perspective. Show me how to live it!
Opening Prayer	Holy Spirit, take me ever deeper into the Mystery. Transform me in the fires of Divine Love.
1st Reading	Holy Spirit, help me to see this in light of the liturgical season and the Sunday "Compass Points." Let this liturgy become a lived experience in my life.
Responsorial Psalm	The response should be my response to the 1st Reading. Am I responding appropriately to God's call in the 1st Reading?
2nd Reading	What deep formation is taking place here?
Gospel Acclamation	How am I being prepared for the Gospel?
Gospel	See this in light of the liturgical season and the Sunday "Compass Points." How am I going to live the Gospel in my daily life?
Prayer over the gifts	How am I offering myself to love this liturgy in the spirit of Our Lady?
Communion Antiphon	How is this lifting up my spirit to live the Eucharist I receive?
Closing Prayer	How am I going forth as a sent person to live this liturgy empowered by the Eucharist?

- **Sunday Compass Points** give lights (insights) into where God will be forming us during that week. We need to know the previous Sunday's liturgy and the next Sunday's liturgy because we are given "Compass Points" for our life. Sunday Compass Points keep us from wandering aimlessly through the week. They give us direction. Our direction is heaven, and Our Lady will help us go in the right direction when we understand that "Liturgy is Life!"

- The **Entrance Antiphon** is an entrance into the mystery of our life. That is what it means. Entrance—we are to enter into the liturgy that is our life. We want to hear this antiphon from God's perspective. We are entering into the mystery of our life in Christ.

- The **Opening Prayer** is so rich. It is a petition for us, given by Christ (the Priest) to the Father, in the Holy Spirit. The words proclaim what Jesus is asking God the Father to give us. And our Good Father will respond to the prayer of Christ.

- The **Readings** unfold this Mystery of Christ. The readings all have specific meaning within the liturgy. The Holy Spirit did not just put them together haphazardly. Everything has an order and a purpose.

- The **First Reading** is proclaimed, then followed by a **Responsorial Psalm**. It is called a Responsorial Psalm because the response is supposed to be our response to the First Reading. Our hearts and spirits should be moved to respond to God's Word in a certain way.

- The **Second Reading**—along with the other readings and homily—can provide us insight into how we can handle the trials, temptations, persecutions and struggles (**TTPS**) that we will face during that week. These **TTPS** are going to happen in your life, but don't worry about them because they all point to grace. You see, grace is invisible. Grace is little like the mustard seed, but it is powerful because it gives life. It is the life of God. We are used to seeing visible things in our existence. So we can see a trial, temptation, persecution or struggle. We can identify them very easily, but don't get caught up in them. They are allowed by God because they point to grace. The **TTPS** remind us, "The grace is here!" They are like red flags alerting us that grace is available. Ask Our Blessed Mother (who is full of grace) how to see the grace, how to find the grace, and how to respond to the grace. This grace is like a pearl of great price in your life. When you learn to grab hold of the grace in all circumstances, your life will be blessed indeed. The Second Reading takes us deeper into the mystery of Christ that is unfolding.

- The **Gospel Acclamation** acclaims where we are going.

- The **Gospel** is an encounter with Christ—an encounter with the *living* Lord Jesus Christ. Scripture is not just a historical book, but one in which we encounter the *living* Word of God that has *real-life* application today! Jesus is alive, and we want to encounter the living Lord Jesus Christ. One encounter with the living Lord Jesus can transform your life as it did with St. Mary Magdalene, and as it did with St. Paul. God is the formator. And

He is forming us in the liturgy so that we can help others have a living encounter with Jesus Christ. Then they can also become the saints that they were created to be. You can become a saint. One encounter with the living Lord Jesus Christ will change your life. And that can happen in every liturgy.

- The **Homily** gives us insight into the mystery of Christ and our call to live this mystery.

- The **Prayer Over the Gifts** shows us how to offer ourselves this week in love.

- The celebration of the **Holy Eucharist** empowers us to live this mystery of Christ. We receive the power of the Most Holy Eucharist to help us live that week in Christ, to become another Christ, and to live our baptism. That is where we will be formed, and where we will be challenged.

- The **Communion Antiphon** and the **Closing Prayer** both identify where God will be working in our life that week.

God's Lessons and Tests

God gives us lessons in each liturgy of the Catholic Mass. And God tests His children. But His testing must be understood properly, for He tests us to prove us. God knows the quality of gold before it goes into the fire. And He proves the quality of the gold during the way of the cross. We are His children. He knows that we are His children, so one can imagine that He calls all of heaven together and says, "Look at my child." And then all the angels and saints of heaven look at you, support you, and cheer you on. Our Father wants us to grow to the full measure of the mature Christ. So in His loving care, He teaches us in the liturgy, then proves us in our daily experiences that follow.

Reflect on the words, "Liturgy is Life!" What does that mean to me?

DAY ONE – Imitating Mary in Living the Liturgy

Our Lady gave her "Fiat!" and then she continued to ponder the message of the Angel Gabriel deep within her heart. We are privileged to have her "Magnificat" recorded for us in Sacred Scripture. We are called to live this hymn of praise to the Most Holy Trinity, by living Our Lady's life every day. As we pray with the Church in the Liturgy of the Hours, we sing the "Magnificat" along with Our Lady. Please pray through this beautiful hymn of praise and ponder its meaning in your own heart:

> *And Mary said, "My soul proclaims the greatness of the Lord, my spirit rejoices in God my Savior for He has looked with favor on His lowly servant. From this day all generations will call me blessed: the Almighty has done great things for me, and Holy is His Name. He has mercy on those who fear Him in every generation. He has shown the strength of His arm, He has scattered the proud in their conceit. He has cast down the mighty from their thrones, and has lifted up the lowly. He has filled the hungry with good things, and the rich He has sent away empty. He has come to the help of His servant Israel for He has remembered His promise of mercy, the*

promise He made to our fathers, to Abraham and his children forever" (Luke 1:46-55).

How will we live this song of Our Lady? How will it make a difference in our life?

DAY TWO – Becoming Like Jesus in Living the Liturgy

God speaks to His children in many ways. But He speaks with great clarity and precision through the liturgy. This shouldn't surprise us. After all, Jesus Christ is the Eternal Word spoken of the Father to all of mankind. *In the beginning was the Word, and the Word was with God and the Word was God (John 1:1).* Jesus also says of Himself, *"I am the way, and the truth, and the life; no one comes to the Father, but by me" (John 14:6).* So if we want to know which "Way" to go, to understand the "Truth," and to live the "Life" of holiness, the best place to start is the liturgy, our gift from the Catholic Church.

Please take the time (today if you are able) to read through the Mass readings for this coming Sunday. You can find these readings in a Sunday Missal, in the *Magnificat* periodical, or online at www.usccb.org. You may utilize the "Liturgy Preparation Chart" as a guide. The following questions may also help as you discern what God has planned for you this week:

- What do I suspect the graces and challenges of this week to be? Where will I be formed this week according to this week's liturgy?

- Are there any possible challenges that seem suited to me?

- Do I foresee a need for special tactics in overcoming some of these challenges?

- How will these truths revealed in the liturgy change the way I react and interact with others this week?

Let us pray:

Dear Father, Son and Holy Spirit, I want to live the liturgy. Give me the resolve to prepare well each week for the Holy Sacrifice of the Mass, so that I may be open and aware of the graces you want to give me. Help me to be constant in my commitment to the daily readings, and to attend daily Mass whenever you allow me to do so. I ask the Blessed Mother to pray for me that I will learn to ponder the great things of God in my heart as she did. I want to live the liturgy, Lord. Please grant me the grace I need to do it! I ask all of this in the Name of the Father and of the Son and of the Holy Spirit. Amen.

DAY THREE – Going Deeper with STMD

Is God calling you deeper? Following are ways to go deeper with Jesus, who calls you to see Him revealed in the Bible (Sacred Scripture), orthodox writings of the saints (faithful witness to Sacred Tradition) and the Catechism (Magisterium's faithful exposition of the Deposit of Faith)—STMD.

Jesus, I know You are the answer to all of my questions. Please reveal yourself to me in Sacred Scripture:

For the word of God is living and active, sharper than any two-edged sword, piercing to the division of soul and spirit, of joints and marrow, and discerning the

thoughts and intentions of the heart (Hebrews 4:12).

He has filled the hungry with good things, and the rich

he has sent away empty (Luke 1:53).

Memorize the above passages from Scripture, turn them over in your mind and let them sink into your soul. What is God telling you here? Am I hungry for His Word, or is my soul too full of other things? Am I being sent away empty?

Feel free to find these passages in your Bible and read them in context. You may even want to read them once silently and then out loud. Spend some time thinking about them, and then take them to prayer. It is always a good idea to memorize verses of Sacred Scripture and make them your own. This is just another way to know Jesus (Who is the Eternal Word) a little better.

Jesus, I know You are the answer to all of my questions. Please reveal yourself to me in the orthodox writings of the saints, which provide a faithful witness to Sacred Tradition.

St. Augustine, that great Doctor of the Church, says the following about the liturgy in his *Confessions*:

> "How I wept, deeply moved by your hymns, songs, and the
> voices that echoed through your Church! What emotion
> I experienced in them! Those sounds flowed into my
> ears, distilling the truth in my heart. A feeling of devotion
> surged within me, and tears streamed down my face—
> tears that did me good."

You might want to know more about the saint who is quoted above. A Weekday Missal is a great place to start when you want to know more about certain saints. And there are many good resources on the internet and in the library about great saints.

Jesus, I know You are the answer to all of my questions. Please reveal yourself to me in the Magisterium's faithful exposition of the Deposit of Faith.

You can turn to the *Catechism of the Catholic Church,* number 1071:

> "As the work of Christ, liturgy is also an action of his *Church*. It makes the Church present and manifests her as the visible sign of the communion in Christ between God and men. It engages the faithful in the new life of the community and involves the 'conscious, active, and fruitful participation' of everyone." (SC 11)

You may want to read more about the topic of the liturgy in Part Two of the *Catechism*, The Celebration of the Christian Mystery, beginning with number 1061.

Use this space to write down any additional thoughts, prayers or epiphanies the Lord has given you during this teaching in your spiritual formation:

Chapter Eight

"How do I live the Mass?"

People are asking, "How do I live the Mass?" The answer is: "Jesus." Let us begin now by praying the "Our Father" along with Jesus, Who glorifies the Father in the Mass:

In the name of the Father and of the Son and of the Holy Spirit. Amen.

Our Father who art in heaven, hallowed be Thy Name. Thy Kingdom come. Thy will be done, on earth as it is in heaven. Give us this day our daily bread, and forgive us our trespasses, as we forgive those who trespass against us, and lead us not into temptation, but deliver us from evil. Amen.

Our Lady of the Most Holy Trinity, pray for us.

In the name of the Father and of the Son and of the Holy Spirit. Amen.

This prayer to Our Father perfectly relates to our formation regarding the Holy Sacrifice of the Mass. As we come to recognize God as Our Father, Our Lady helps us relate to God as Our Father. We realize that we were created out of Trinitarian love. In the Mass (through the power of the Holy Spirit) we come together as Church, as God's family. That is why we gather for the Mass. We are a family. We come together around the Eucharistic altar and table to remember, to be strengthened, and to go forward. The word Mass comes from "mission." At the end of each Mass, the priest sends us on a mission as He says, "Let us go in peace to love and serve the Lord." We reply, "Thanks be to God." We should take this call to love and serve God and His people very seriously. For in our response, we have just consented to the "mission" at hand and we are thanking God for sending us forth!

In the Mass, we glorify the Father in offering the perfect worship of Jesus' *one* Sacrifice of Calvary. As Scripture makes clear, this sacrifice did not begin and end on the Cross, but rather culminated in everlasting glory in the heavenly sanctuary at Jesus' Ascension (*CCC* 662; cf. numbers 1137-39). Jesus doesn't *need* our assistance; but He and the Father enable us to participate in His one offering, to offer fitting worship through the power of the Holy Spirit despite our littleness and our sinfulness. In the Mass, Christ serves as the "high priest of the New Covenant" (*CCC* 1348). In the Old Covenant Passover, you not only offered a *lamb* but consumed it as well. In the New Covenant Passover, the Mass, we offer and partake of *the Lamb of God*, Jesus Christ (cf. *CCC* 1340, 1362-65). In addition, in the Old Covenant, offerings were made for the imperfect atonement of sins, such as on the annual Day of Atonement. In the New Covenant, because it is the *one, perfect* Sacrifice of Calvary that is made sacramentally present, the offering of the Mass has power to forgive the sins we daily commit (*CCC* 1366; cf. *CCC* 662).

So we go to Mass to glorify the Father and to offer Him everything we have received from Him, to offer ourselves with Jesus as a holy and acceptable sacrifice. The Mass is a sacrifice of love, from which flows our sanctification. In this sanctification, which flows from our offering and partaking of our Eucharistic Lord, we receive the graces from heaven to live holy lives (answering the universal call to holiness).

Many of you have attended Mass far more times than you can count. But the question is, do you really *participate* in the Mass as we are called to do? Do you really *"see"* what is happening in the Mass, or are you just "kind of there"?

The richness and sublimity of the Holy Sacrifice of the Mass transcends all attempts at description. In a word, as noted, the Mass is "perfect." The fact that it is perfect is certainly not owing to human effort. We have all assisted at Mass imperfectly at one time or another. The Mass is perfect, again, because it is the one holy Sacrifice of Calvary, the sacrifice which began on the Cross, continued in the Resurrection and culminated in everlasting glory in the heavenly sanctuary at the Ascension. We become present to and participate in this most sublime offering, in which Jesus offers Himself to the Father in the Holy Spirit. That is, heaven and earth become one in what the Church calls the "heavenly liturgy" (cf. *CCC* 662, 1137-39)! So, in reality, the Mass is a most profound encounter with the High Priest of Heaven in particular and the Trinity in general. Jesus makes up for what is lacking in us, and makes a perfect sacrifice of Himself (on our behalf) to the Father in the Holy Spirit. If we view the Mass from the outside looking in, we are looking from the wrong vantage point.

Remember, we always want to begin at the beginning, with the Alpha and the Omega. We want to begin with God. When we view the Mass from the Trinity's perspective, we begin to see the Father, Son, and the Holy Spirit more clearly, as they truly are in reality. We don't view the Mass from the *outside*, but from the *inside*. We are to "become what we behold." The Mass is not celebrated as something outside of ourselves. It is not a spectator sport. With our eyes, we view space between us and the altar, yet what we see is not all that exists. If we did not know that simple truth with certainty, we could not be followers of Christ.

We can also be certain that our bodies are one with our immortal souls, even though we do not see the soul with our physical eyes. We also know that every person has a Guardian Angel. So for every person that we see, there are twice as many living beings present in that place (than what we see). Similarly when we "see" the Mass, as it truly is, there is vastly more to be perceived with our interior sight than is possible to explain adequately. We can only "see" the Mass when we allow ourselves to be *transformed by the renewal of [our] mind (Romans 12:2)* through the power of the Holy Spirit.

This week, go to Mass with Our Lady, and ask her to help you unite yourself with Jesus and give yourself entirely to Him. Think about how Our Lady gave herself entirely over to the will of God. Think of how she allowed her entire life to be consumed and transformed in the fire of Divine Love. Think about how she allowed herself to be made one with Jesus and offered herself as a loving victim for our sake.

DAY ONE – Imitating Mary in Living the Mass

Our Lady, in addition to being full of grace, exceeded all human persons in every virtue and in possessing the most humble, obedient and loving heart ever to beat within a human frame. This makes perfect sense when you consider that her will was not weakened and her mind not darkened by sin, and that she lived face-to-face with the Incarnate Word for thirty years.

Mary, Our Blessed Mother, sees the Mass from the inside, and she wants her children to see it that way, too. When we begin to imitate Mary's perspective on the Mass, our entire experience of the Holy Sacrifice is transformed. So how does Our Lady view the Mass?

In saying "yes" at the Annunciation, "Mary inaugurates the Church's participation in the sacrifice of the Redeemer" (*Sacramentum Caritatis*, number 33). That is, the "Word" was made Flesh for the very first time within her virginal womb. St. Augustine said that Mary conceived Jesus in her heart before she ever conceived Him in her womb. This profound assent to God's will that occurred in Mary's heart, even before the Incarnation of Jesus in her body (with her full and unwavering consent in her "Fiat!") is essential to living the Mass. This profound assent also occurs in Mary at the foot of the Cross on Calvary, united in the suffering of her Son to the Father in the Holy Spirit. The Mass is the re-presentation of the one sacrifice of Jesus on Calvary in an unbloody manner (cf. *CCC* 1367). "Unbloody" because Jesus dies only once; yet "re-presentation" because Jesus' sacrifice culminated in everlasting glory in the heavenly sanctuary and thus can be made present on earth *today*. In addition, because Jesus is a Divine Person who is not limited by time, we become mystically *present* to Our Lord's "Paschal Mystery" in general at Mass, including the event of the Cross (cf. *CCC* 1085).

At every Mass, we have the opportunity to emulate Our Blessed Mother to be transformed from within. When we stop limiting ourselves and we open our hearts to the Infinite God, we can allow ourselves to be enveloped, immersed, filled and transformed by the sacred mysteries. Just like Our Blessed Mother, we can then begin to become what we behold.

As our Holy Father, Pope Benedict XVI, so eloquently states:

"Consequently, every time we approach the Body and Blood of Christ in the Eucharistic liturgy, we also turn to her who, by her complete fidelity, received Christ's sacrifice for the whole Church."[18] He goes on to say that Our Mother "is the Immaculata, who receives God's gift unconditionally and is thus associated by the work of salvation. Mary of Nazareth, icon of the nascent *(developing)* Church, is the model for each of us, called to receive the gift that Jesus makes of himself in the Eucharist."[19]

Obviously, we are not talking about externals. We know that in the Church each sacrament shows us the "visible sign of the hidden reality of salvation."[20] We are not considering what we see with our eyes. Rather, we are touching on a fraction of what our interior can experience in the Mass.

"We fulfill [our essential part in the Mass] when we do actually make ourselves one with Jesus; one with him in his act of love; one

18 Pope Benedict XVI, *Sacramentum Caritatis*, No. 33.
19 Pope Benedict XVI, *Sacramentum Caritatis*, No. 33.
20 *Catechism of the Catholic Church*, 774.

with him in his role of victim."

What does it mean to be a victim? It means to lay ourselves upon the altar of God's will. It means to say to God, from the heart's deepest abyss, "Take me, God. I am all yours. Do what you want with me. To love and to labor or to suffer and to die; it is all the same to me, just so your will is done in me. Make me an instrument for the doing of your work. Fit me into your plan no matter how hard you may have to hit to hammer me into place."[21]

- Do I have reservations about becoming a "victim" as Our Lord and Our Lady were "victims"?

- How will I strive to unite myself (as Mary did) with Jesus this week in the Mass?

Pope Benedict XVI further illuminates these points when he says that the faithful should:

> "...take part in the Eucharistic liturgy not 'as strangers or silent spectators', but as participants 'in the sacred action, conscious of what they are doing, actively and devoutly'.... They should give thanks to God. Offering the immaculate Victim, not only through the hands of the priest but also together with him, **they should learn to make an offering of themselves. Through Christ, the Mediator, they should be drawn day by day into ever more perfect union with God and each other.**"[22]

- -

21 Fr. Leo Trese, *The Faith Explained*, pg. 408.
22 Pope Benedict XVI, *Sacramentum Caritatis*, No. 52 [emphasis added].

- How will I make an offering of myself this week?

- What can I do to work toward "ever more perfect union with God" and my community?

DAY TWO – Becoming Like Jesus in Living the Mass

Now consider the fourfold purpose of the Mass:

- To adore God

- To thank God

- To petition God for grace

- To atone to God for sin

"As we assist at Mass, this fourfold purpose [of adoration, thanksgiving, petition and atonement] should be primary in our intentions as we offer the Holy Sacrifice."[23]

Sometimes, we are tempted to think of Mass in this way, "What is in it for me?" While it is true that Our Lord profusely showers graces upon us during Mass, "God's glory must have precedence over the graces the Mass brings to us."[24]

After all these considerations, we come back to the central point: How does Our Lord want us to see the Mass? What does the One High Priest and Spotless Victim say to us regarding the Mass?

At the very first Mass (the Last Supper) Jesus said to His Disciples, *"This is my body which is given for you. Do this in remembrance*

---

23 Fr. Leo Trese, *The Faith Explained*, pg. 382.
24 Fr. Leo Trese, *The Faith Explained*, pg. 382.

of me" (Luke 22:19). So Our Lord is asking that we celebrate the Mass in order to remember Him in a very special way. As always, His gifts exceed our greatest expectations, and the Mass is certainly no exception. As Jesus served as Priest and Victim at the Last Supper, He also conferred the Holy Priesthood upon the Apostles. So now we can begin to understand how Jesus wants us to view the Mass.

First of all, the Mass is a memorial or remembrance of Our Lord. *"Do this,"* Jesus says as He makes His Apostles Priests of the New and Everlasting Covenant, *"in remembrance of me."* It is natural for us to desire a fresh memory of those whom we have loved and admired (from photographs to mementos and keepsakes). The world is filled with such remembrances. But liturgical remembrance is much deeper. This remembrance is "not merely a recollection of past events" and experiences, as seen in the events of Scripture. Rather, these events and experiences "become in a certain way present and real" because of the participation of God, who is not limited by time (*CCC* 1363). This was true in the Old Covenant Passover and much more profoundly so in the New Covenant Passover: "When the Church celebrates the Eucharist, she commemorates Christ's Passover, and it is made present: the sacrifice Christ offered once for all on the cross remains ever present" (*CCC* 1364, cf. Heb 7:25-27). "Our Lord Jesus who loves us so, and who wants our love so much, has left us a memorial of Himself such as only God could fashion. It is not a picture, not a monument or statue— *it is a living presence of Himself, coming daily among us in the Mass.* In addition to being a remembrance of Our Lord, the Mass is a holy banquet. At his table, Jesus feeds us with his own body and blood."[25]

So Our Lord wants us to remember Him. He wants us to realize that He is truly coming to us, and that He is fully present to us, Body, Blood, Soul and Divinity—really, truly and substantially present. It is a "Feast of Love," given for the benefit of each and all who worthily approach in faith.

Our Lord calls each of us by name and sends us a personal invitation to this Feast of Love. He wants us to take the Mass personally—very personally—as it is a living encounter with Him. It is amazing to think that Jesus would make this sacrifice for just one of us, but that is true. Jesus offered Himself for you, and He wants you to know that and to take the Mass very personally.

So both individually and collectively, we are one in the Body of Christ. As a part of the indivisible Body of Christ, **"We are asking rather that we ourselves might become a Eucharist with Christ and, thus, become acceptable and pleasing to God." We are to "become one with Him in a single spiritual life."**[26] An absolutely profound statement from Joseph Cardinal Ratzinger, the future Pope Benedict XVI: **"We are to become one with Him in a single spiritual life."**

- Have you ever considered what it means to have a real share in Christ's own spiritual life?

- How does this challenge the way you view your own spirituality?

. . . .

25 Fr. Leo Trese, *The Faith Explained*, pgs. 372–373 [emphasis added].
26 Joseph Cardinal Ratzinger, *Pilgrim Fellowship of Faith: The Church as Communion*, p. 116 [emphasis added].

If we can understand the Mass as sharing fully in the spiritual life of Jesus Christ, our lives will be changed and we will experience the Mass as a living encounter with Christ.

Looking through, with, and in the eyes of Jesus in the Mass (as we "present our bodies as a living sacrifice") we undergo a metamorphosis, and are reshaped in a way that takes us beyond this world's scheme of things—beyond sharing in what people think and say and do, and into the will of God. "The bodies—that is, the bodily persons—that become a Eucharist **no longer stand alongside each other but become one with and one in the one Body and in the one living Christ.**"[27]

- How does this knowledge of being one with the Church and Christ Himself impact our prayer life? Do you feel a sense of urgency for the needs of the other members of the Body?

As we look with the eyes of Jesus at the Mass, we see His ultimate goal for us—communion. He made us for Himself and He wants us completely (all of us) in full and total communion with the Trinity. What a glorious gift!

- How does the knowledge that Jesus wishes to possess us completely affect you?

- Do you believe that there are certain parts of your life that are "off-limits," even to Him?

- How will you extend yourself to Him and allow Him to trans-

27 Joseph Cardinal Ratzinger, *Pilgrim Fellowship of Faith: The Church as Communion*, pgs. 117–119 [emphasis added].

form you and renew your mind so that you may live in the will
of God and become good, pleasing and perfect in the eyes of
the Father?

Meditate on the above questions and journal your answers. These
questions should make us go deeper—don't be surprised at what
you find there. God is not afraid of your answers, and He will always
meet you where you are in His unending love and infinite mercy. You
can always be honest with Him for He alone knows your heart. He
is waiting for you to come to Him with all of yourself. Will you deny
Him? Or will you give Him what is rightfully His?

The following prayer is a prayer of spiritual communion. Many
Catholics are familiar with this type of prayer, as it is what you should
pray many times each day, especially if you cannot attend daily Mass.
You can also pray it to increase your fervor.

**A partial indulgence may be obtained if this particular
prayer is repeated three times, so we recommend that you
triple it.**

> *O Jesus, I turn toward the holy tabernacle where You
> live hidden for me. I love You, O my God. I cannot
> receive You in Holy Communion. Come, nevertheless,
> and visit me with Your grace. Come spiritually into my
> heart. Purify it. Sanctify it. Render it like unto Your
> own. Amen.*

DAY THREE – Going Deeper with STMD

Is God calling you deeper? Following are ways to go deeper with

Jesus, who calls you to see Him revealed in the Bible (Sacred Scripture), orthodox writings of the saints (faithful witness to Sacred Tradition) and the Catechism (Magisterium's faithful exposition of the Deposit of Faith)—STMD.

Jesus, I know You are the answer to all of my questions. Please reveal yourself to me in Sacred Scripture:

> *I appeal to you therefore, brethren, by the mercies of God, to present your bodies as a living sacrifice, holy and acceptable to God, which is your spiritual worship (Romans 12:1).*

> *Do not be conformed to this world but be transformed by the renewal of your mind, that you may prove what is the will of God, what is good and acceptable and perfect (Romans 12:2).*

What does it mean to present your very own body as a "living sacrifice"? Is doing this going to change the way you live your daily life?

Feel free to find these passages in your Bible and read them in context. You may even want to read them once silently and then out loud. Spend some time thinking about them, and then take them to prayer. It is always a good idea to memorize verses of Sacred Scripture and make them your own. This is just another way to know Jesus (Who is the Eternal Word) a little better.

Jesus, I know You are the answer to all of my questions. Please reveal yourself to me in the orthodox writings of the saints, which provide a faithful witness to Sacred Tradition.

St. Padre Pio has this to say about the *Mass*:

> "The earth could exist more easily without the sun than
> without the Holy Mass. If we only knew how God regards
> this sacrifice, we would risk our lives to be present at a
> single Mass. Renew your faith by attending Holy Mass.
> Keep your mind focused on the Mystery unfolding before
> your eyes. In your mind's eye transport yourself to Calvary
> and meditate on the Victim who offers Himself to Divine
> Justice, paying the price of your redemption."

You might want to know more about the saint who is quoted
above. A Weekday Missal is a great place to start when you want to
know more about certain saints. And there are many good resources
on the internet and in the library about great saints.

Jesus, I know You are the answer to all of my questions. Please
reveal yourself to me in the Magisterium's faithful exposition of the
Deposit of Faith.

You can turn to the *Catechism of the Catholic Church,*
Part Two:

The Mass of all ages

1345 As early as the second century we have the witness
of St. Justin Martyr for the basic lines of the order of the
Eucharistic celebration. They have stayed the same until
our own day for all the great liturgical families. St. Justin
wrote to the pagan emperor Antoninus Pius (138-161)
around the year 155, explaining what Christians did:

On the day we call the day of the sun, all who dwell in the city or country gather in the same place.

The memoirs of the apostles and the writings of the prophets are read, as much as time permits.

When the reader has finished, he who presides over those gathered admonishes and challenges them to imitate these beautiful things.

Then we all rise together and offer prayers for ourselves...and for all others, wherever they may be, so that we may be found righteous by our life and actions, and faithful to the commandments, so as to obtain eternal salvation.

When the prayers are concluded we exchange the kiss.

Then someone brings bread and a cup of water and wine mixed together to him who presides over the brethren.

He takes them and offers praise and glory to the Father of the universe, through the name of the Son and of the Holy Spirit and for a considerable time he gives thanks (in Greek: *eucharistian*) that we have been judged worthy of these gifts.

When he has concluded the prayers and thanksgivings, all present give voice to an acclamation by saying: "Amen."

When he who presides has given thanks and the people have responded, those whom we call deacons give to those present the "eucharisted" bread, wine and water and take them to those who are absent. (St. Justin, *Apol.* 1, 65-67: PG 6, 428-429; the text before the asterisk (*) is from chap. 67)

1346 The liturgy of the Eucharist unfolds according to a fundamental structure which has been preserved throughout the centuries down to our own day. It displays two great parts that form a fundamental unity:

– the gathering, the liturgy of the Word, with readings, homily and general intercessions;

– the liturgy of the Eucharist, with the presentation of the bread and wine, the consecratory thanksgiving, and communion.

The liturgy of the Word and liturgy of the Eucharist together form "one single act of worship;" (SC 56) the Eucharistic table set for us is the table both of the Word of God and of the Body of the Lord. (Cf. *Dei Verbum* 21)

1347 Is this not the same movement as the Paschal meal of the risen Jesus with his disciples? Walking with them he explained the Scriptures to them; sitting with them at table "he took bread, blessed and broke it, and gave it to them." (Cf. Lk 24:13-35)

You may want to read more about the topic of the Mass in Part Two of the *Catechism*, The Celebration of the Christian Mystery, under the heading: The Sacrament of the Eucharist, see numbers 1322-1419.

Use this space to write down any additional thoughts, prayers or epiphanies the Lord has given you during this teaching in your spiritual formation:

Chapter Nine

"How do I live the Truth in Sacred Scripture, Sacred Tradition and the Magisterium's faithful exposition of the Deposit of Faith?"

People are asking, "How do I live the Truth present in Sacred Scripture, Sacred Tradition and the Magisterium's faithful exposition of the Deposit of Faith?" The answer is: "Jesus." Let us begin by praying the "Our Father" along with Jesus, from Whom we have received Sacred Scripture, Sacred Tradition and the Magisterium, which faithfully expounds the Deposit of Faith:

In the name of the Father and of the Son and of the Holy Spirit. Amen.

Our Father who art in heaven, hallowed be Thy Name. Thy Kingdom come. Thy will be done, on earth as it is in heaven. Give us this day our daily bread, and forgive us our trespasses, as we forgive those who trespass against us, and lead us not into temptation, but deliver us from evil. Amen.

Our Lady of the Most Holy Trinity, pray for us.

In the name of the Father and of the Son and of the Holy Spirit. Amen.

Our formation continues today by talking about Sacred Scripture (the written books of the Bible), Sacred Tradition (the Gospel handed on orally to and through the Apostles), and the Church's Magisterium (which faithfully expounds the Deposit of Faith).

As noted at the beginning of this formation program, God's Word is transmitted to us in Sacred Scripture and Sacred Tradition, which collectively contain the "Deposit of Faith" that the Magisterium faithfully expounds in providing us with the Church's teachings on faith and morals. The Magisterium is the Church's teaching office and is comprised of the Pope and the bishops in communion with him.

This is one of the most important teachings along the path of your conversion. It is necessary to embrace these three inseparable gifts in order to live the faith in total surrender to God (which is the call of Jesus on the way to the truth and life that He won for us). Yes, Jesus came to give us life, abundant life and eternal life. We are all so fortunate to be members of the Catholic Church, where we have the fullness of faith. St. Cyril of Alexandria said:

"The Catholic Church is the distinctive name of this holy Church which is the mother of us all. She is the bride of Our Lord Jesus Christ, the only-begotten Son of God, for Scripture says: *Christ loved the Church and gave Himself up for her.* She is the type and she bears the image of the Jerusalem above that is free and is the mother of us all, that Jerusalem that once was barren but now has many children."

As members of the Catholic Church, we have over one billion brothers and sisters. A Catholic author expressed, "Holy Church is my Mother, to feed me, rear me, and lead me to heaven." We are so blessed to have such a Mother to feed us, rear us and lead us to heaven. We know that Jesus Himself founded the Church, first entrusting the keys of the Kingdom to Saint Peter. And the succession has continued unbroken until the present day. What a gift from the Heart of Jesus! Only the Church established by Jesus Christ could have stood firm against so many attacks for over 2,000 years.

Sacred Scripture, Sacred Tradition and the Magisterium of the Church (through her faithful exposition of the Deposit of Faith) are the three, indivisible elements that ensure we are well fed, properly reared, and safely led to heaven. There is no way to separate the three for they are inextricably bound together. Sacred Scripture and Sacred Tradition transmit Revelation, and the Magisterium's faithful exposition of the Deposit of Faith gives us the proper understanding of Revelation.

If God did not expressly reveal Himself to us, we would all remain in the dark. Think about the mystery of the Holy Trinity, for instance. What if God had never expressly revealed the mystery of the Trinity through Sacred Tradition and Sacred Scripture? Our minds would never have been able to understand the concept of Three Persons in One God. Even the brightest person must admit that God is indeed a mystery, and for us to grasp His Majesty He must expressly reveal Himself to us (Divine Revelation).

You need to know that Sacred Scripture came from Apostolic Tradition, which is inclusive of both Scripture and Sacred Tradition, and that the canon of Scripture was gifted to the world by the Catholic Church. **There would not be a New Testament were it not for the Catholic Church.** The regional Council of Rome under Pope Damasus settled the New Testament—and the canon of Scripture in general—in 382 A.D. The Council of Trent later provided a dogmatic definition on the matter in the 1500s, when Martin Luther and others disputed the canon.

Some Christians reduce God's Word to "Scripture alone," saying all they need in being disciples of Jesus Christ is the Bible. Yet, *someone* must authoritatively interpret the Bible when there are doctrinal disagreements, and many people in recent centuries have attempted to fulfill a teaching role which God has given only to the Church's Magisterium. The practical result is that today there are thousands and thousands of *different* Protestant denominations in the world. In other words, various persons have attempted to fulfill the Magisterium's role and the result has been many conflicting denominations, a climate of division that God never intended.

On the other hand, there are professed Catholics who ardently profess that they believe in Scripture, Sacred Tradition and the Magisterium's faithful exposition of the Deposit of Faith, yet they don't submit to the authority of the Magisterium in *current times*. They veer off in one dissenting direction or another, from those who believe that they can override official Church teaching via "the primacy of their conscience," to those who basically think they're "more Catholic than the Pope," and who thus go the way of schism or even "sedevacantism," which means they don't believe the current Pope is validly elected.

This is why it's crucial for us to be properly rooted "STMD Catholics," Catholics who recognize Scripture, Tradition and the Deposit of Faith, but precisely as faithfully safeguarded and expounded by the successor of Peter, the Pope, and the bishops in communion with him; that is, by the authentic Magisterium.

Let us now review this beautiful trilogy of Truth through the eyes of Our Lady. We look through Our Lady because she always looks at the Church (the Mystical Body of Christ Her Son) with the eyes of a daughter, a spouse, a mother and a disciple.

Because of Mary's profound humility, she was the first recipient of God's expressed Revelation about the Incarnation of Christ. If we want to fully receive the manifold gifts of God through the Church, we must learn to be humble like Our Lady. We must open our hands and hearts to receive her gifts. Our Lady teaches us how to trust the Church. She always believed in God's plan for her life, and she always, in her profound humility, accepted everything as a gift from His hand. She never asked for detailed explanations. She just heard, listened, pondered, believed and lived.

Mary lived her faith perfectly. She was the first to receive Jesus in the flesh. She was the chosen Spouse and Sanctuary of the Holy Spirit of God. She was the Mother of the Word made Flesh. She is also Jesus' first and best disciple, and the Mother of the Church. All of this was ordained by God from the beginning of time, and facilitated by Our Lady's humble receptivity, sensitive docility, and total self-surrender to the will of the Father for her entire life.

Looking at Our Lady, we easily see that humility, docility and self-surrender allowed her to bear the perfect fruit: Jesus. Our Mother had prepared her heart, her mind—her very being all her life. She had studied, lived and embraced the Hebrew Scriptures since she was a little child. She knew, loved, and trusted God through her life of prayer and Scripture study before the Angel Gabriel ever came to announce that she would be the Mother of God. She was a true, loyal, devout, and loving daughter of the Father before she ever became the mother of God the Son, by the power of the Holy Spirit. As noted before, St. Augustine said that Our Lady conceived in her heart before she conceived in her womb.

All the many days, months and years of prayer and study prepared her soul to receive Him. This demonstrates something very important to all of us who are Her children. Mary is Our Mother and our Model in Faith. If she devoted herself so eagerly to prayer and study, then we should follow her example. Our Lady was open and she said "yes" to the plan of God. She did not say, "Prove it to me." She did not say, "I have my own ideas." She did not set herself up as the sole authority of the understanding of the Revelation of God. She was open to the Revelation of God. She trusted in God and she related to God. Because of her humility, the Word became Flesh and dwelt among us.

So how do we imitate Our Lady's humility, docility and self-surrender to the will of the Father? One very concrete and straightforward way is to simply believe everything the Catholic Church proposes for our belief. We can begin to imitate Our Lady in earnest when we let go of our own petty notions and prideful ideas and trust the Church in everything.

If this seems radical to you, then you are normal, for it is radical. Being a follower of Jesus Christ in the school of Mary is a radical calling. But it is the only way to receive the complete freedom needed to open yourself to the full Revelation of God, and allow Jesus to be "spiritually conceived" fully in your very own life. Do you want to conceive Jesus fully in your life in this way? Do you want the fruitfulness in Jesus to come forth in your life, in your family, in your workplace, and in every life you touch? Then remain open to the full Revelation of God, by staying open to the Magisterium of the Catholic Church.

Some people struggle with complete obedience to various teachings of the Church. Some people pick and choose what they apply to their lives. Unfortunately, this approach does not bear good fruit. "To give *selective assent* to the teachings of the Church deprives us of her life-giving message, but also seriously endangers our communion with her" (Excerpted from: *Happy Are Those Who Are Called to His Supper*, USCCB 2006—emphasis added).

We often find people who are convinced that they have superior insight to that of the Church. When they come up against a teaching that seems challenging or uncomfortable, they usually say, "You know, sometimes the *Catechism* just seems a little out of touch. It's not really meant for those of us who are living in the modern world." Or at other times they say, "This Scripture sounds really harsh. I can't imagine that God expects such high standards from us today," or "This was all well and good for St. Augustine, but he's a saint! Certainly this doesn't apply to me." The problems with these statements are vast, but they all stem from the same source: these statements all start with "me," and not with God. They all begin from my point of view and not His.

God does not ask us to do something unless He makes it possible. With God, all things are possible. If we want to bear much fruit (like Our Lady), we must begin with God. We must be willing to abandon our sometimes narrow-minded and often prideful thinking, and allow the Church to teach us through Sacred Scripture, Sacred Tradition and the Magisterium's faithful exposition of the Deposit of Faith. If we start tearing out the pages that we don't agree with or don't like, then we do not have God's Word—we have *our word*. As St. Augustine said, "If you believe what you like in the Gospels, and reject what you don't like, it is not the Gospel you believe, but yourself."

People often say they have a "problem with authority." Really, what they often mean is that they have a problem with unjust authority, or the misuse of authority. Having been mistreated or misguided by "human" authority through a boss who was unjust or a parent who was abusive, some of us have developed certain defense mechanisms that make us want to bristle under any kind of perceived authority.

But Jesus came to show us that authority is supposed to be exercised in complete mercy and never-ending love. This is proper authority—authority we can trust. This is the authority of the Church. This authority keeps us safe from harm and sets us free to be the person we were created to be (made in the image and likeness of God). In imitation of Our Lady, when we submit to the authority of the Church in all things, we are open to the Revelation of Almighty God, and then we will bear much fruit.

DAY ONE – Imitating Mary Through Embracing STMD

Ask Mary to give you her perfect heart as you ponder Sacred Scripture, the saints' faithful witness to Sacred Tradition and the Magisterium's faithful exposition of the Deposit of Faith. Letting go of your own ideas about how things should be can be very difficult. But God wants you to trust Him completely. And Our Lady knows how to say "Yes!" to God without hesitation, because she trusts Him completely, and knows that He loves her perfectly. She wants to teach you how to trust and know Him, too.

Our Lady, as Queen of heaven and earth, sees the Church Militant (that's all of us fighting the good fight here on earth) all at once. She is the Mother of the Church, and she loves each of us with an unending, ever-merciful love. She desires for each one of us to be free and completely open to God's Word as gifted to us in Sacred Scripture, Sacred Tradition and the Magisterium's faithful exposition of the Deposit of Faith. As we have said, humility is the necessary disposition to all growth in holiness. Actually, humility is a true gauge of our openness to the Revelation and love of God. Therefore, please take a moment to pray the Litany of Humility, and ponder in your heart how to more fully open yourself to God's Truth, and to embrace the gifts offered to you in Sacred Scripture, Sacred Tradition and the Magisterium's faithful exposition of the Deposit of Faith.

Litany of Humility

~Rafael Cardinal Merry del Val

O Jesus, meek and humble of heart, hear me.

From the desire of being esteemed, *deliver me, Jesus.*
From the desire of being loved, *deliver me, Jesus.*
From the desire of being extolled, *deliver me, Jesus.*
From the desire of being honored, *deliver me, Jesus.*
From the desire of being praised, *deliver me, Jesus.*
From the desire of being preferred to others, *deliver me, Jesus.*
From the desire of being consulted, *deliver me, Jesus.*
From the desire of being approved, *deliver me, Jesus.*
From the fear of being humiliated, *deliver me, Jesus.*

From the fear of being despised, *deliver me, Jesus.*

From the fear of suffering rebukes, *deliver me, Jesus.*

From the fear of being calumniated, *deliver me, Jesus.*

From the fear of being forgotten, *deliver me, Jesus.*

From the fear of being ridiculed, *deliver me, Jesus.*

From the fear of being wronged, *deliver me, Jesus.*

From the fear of being suspected, *deliver me, Jesus.*

That others may be loved more than I,

    Jesus, grant me the grace to desire it.

That others may be esteemed more than I,

    Jesus, grant me the grace to desire it.

That in the opinion of the world, others may increase and I may

    decrease, *Jesus, grant me the grace to desire it.*

That others may be chosen and I set aside,

    Jesus, grant me the grace to desire it.

That others may be praised and I unnoticed,

    Jesus, grant me the grace to desire it.

That others may be preferred to me in everything,

    Jesus, grant me the grace to desire it.

That others may become holier than I, provided that I may become as

    holy as I should, *Jesus, grant me the grace to desire it.* Amen.

Blessed Mother, please teach me to be open to the Revelation
of God and to ponder His Word in my heart. Please ask Our Lord to
increase my faith in Him and perfect my trust in His Church. Amen.

    But Mary kept all these things, pondering them in her heart
(Luke 2:19).

DAY TWO –

Becoming Like Jesus Through Embracing STMD

The Incarnate Word, i.e., the Second Person of the Trinity Who became flesh to reveal God's love to us, moves us to embrace Sacred Scripture, the saints' faithful witness to Sacred Tradition and the Magisterium's faithful exposition of the Deposit of Faith. Divine Revelation is the way God reveals Himself to man, and it has been entrusted to the Catholic Church.

Have you ever thought of why He would do such a thing? Why would the Almighty, Eternal One who created the endless universe decide to reveal Himself to us? He reveals Himself to us because He loves us infinitely, and Love desires to communicate Himself to the Beloved.

In his book *Letter and Spirit: From Written Text to Living Word in the Liturgy*, Scott Hahn explains how the Word of God is transmitted through Scripture in particular:

"Both the Church Fathers and their rabbinic contemporaries spoke of the Scriptures in terms of 'divine accommodation'—God stooping down to communicate with His children on their level, or lifting them up to see from a divine perspective. In the third century, Origen wrote of this as a manifestation of God's fatherhood: 'whenever the divine plan *[oikonomia]* involves human affairs, God takes on human intelligence, manners and language, just as when we talk to a child of two we talk baby-talk.'"[28]

So throughout salvation history, Our Father has been

. . . .

28 Scott Hahn, *Letter and Spirit*, pg. 17.

communicating Himself to us. He has done this in various ways. He has spoken to and through the prophets. He has inspired innumerable writers through the power of the Holy Spirit. And finally, He gave us His only Son, *"and the Word became flesh and dwelt among us."* All these modes and methods of communication point to one thing only—Love. All of Sacred Scripture, Sacred Tradition, and the Magisterium's faithful exposition of the Deposit of Faith point to the one Person of Jesus Christ, the God-Man. Through words, events and actions, God was leading His people to Christ, to the Incarnation of the Word, and on through the Paschal Mystery (the Passion, Death, Resurrection and Ascension of Jesus Christ) which is the source of our Redemption.

How are we to respond to this unfathomable gift? We are to respond the only way one can respond to an outpouring of true, beautiful, perfect love—with love. Our God is so awesome, so beautiful, so unpredictable, and always full of surprises. No one could ever love us like He does. God is pure Goodness, and nothing He does has any bounds—He is infinite. He loves us as only a perfect, good and infinite Father can love us. He will never stop loving us. He will love us for all of eternity. It is only this love that truly satisfies the human heart, and there is no substitute for it. No matter how much other people love us, they cannot ever love us perfectly. Only God (who is perfect) can do that.

In expressing His love, He will always communicate with us, as He has throughout the centuries. Sacred Scripture, also known as the "Holy Bible," is an exalted way in which He communicates his love. The Bible is a beautiful, holy book that tells of God's abiding love for us all. All Catholics who participate in Mass on a regular basis have heard a great deal (if not all) of the Bible proclaimed.

And the Church's Magisterium, as established by Jesus Christ, assures us of the proper understanding of the Bible, and does so in light of how Scripture has been understood in the Church's living Sacred Tradition. (Please review Matthew 16:18-19 and Luke 22:32—St. Peter is given the chief authority to guide the Church in faith and morals; also please review 1 Timothy 3:15—the Catholic Church is called the "pillar and foundation of truth.")

This is an important distinction to clarify to those who ask what purpose Sacred Scripture, Sacred Tradition and the Magisterium serve in the Church. Most of the time, people are just looking for a reasonable explanation, and as Catholics we know that faith and reason go together like hand and glove. So as we hear in 1 Peter, we should *in [our] hearts reverence Christ as Lord* and *Always be prepared to make a defense to any one who calls you to account for the hope that is in you, yet do it with gentleness and reverence; and keep your conscience clear, so that, when you are abused, those who revile your good behavior in Christ may be put to shame. For it is better to suffer for doing right, if that should be God's will, than for doing wrong (1 Peter 3:15-17).* As Catholics, we never use the beautiful Word of God to hurt others. And we do not twist or distort the Word of God to suit our own needs. Rather, we rejoice because the Holy Spirit protects the Magisterium from teaching error regarding Scripture in her faithful exposition of the Deposit of Faith.

After all, isn't the whole point of following Christ to become more like Him? Isn't that the reason you are reading this book? Do you want to live and move and have your being in Him? Do you want to give Him your life and all it contains? If you want to stay humble and put your life at the service of the Bridegroom, then say along with John the Baptist, *"He must increase, but I must decrease" (John 3:30).*

Fr. Leo Trese now shares more wisdom on becoming like Jesus, and how we need to read and know the Bible to do that:

"We say—and we believe—that the essence of Christian living lies in our effort to develop a Christlikeness in ourselves. Our purpose is to make ourselves over in the image of Christ. We want to learn to see life whole as He sees it, and not live our days in fragmented fashion, with our family life, bread-winning work, recreation, social responsibilities, and personal relationships frequently in conflict with one with the other."[29]

We want to become like Jesus in every way. So we must know Him intimately, and to know Him intimately we must read the Bible. The Gospels, the Epistles, the New Testament and the Old Testament all speak of Him in various ways. When we read the Bible, we get to know Jesus even better. And we were put here on this earth "to know, love, and serve Him and be happy with Him forever in heaven." Notice that the knowing comes first.

This perfect Bridegroom made a perfect plan for His bride, the Church. First, He commissioned His Apostles to preach the Gospel or "Good News," making disciples of all nations. Under the guidance of the Holy Spirit whom Jesus sent to aid them, the Apostles then handed on the Gospel or "Apostolic Tradition" both orally and in

. . . .

29 Fr. Leo Trese, *The Faith Explained*, pg. 563.

written form, *i.e.*, via Sacred Tradition and Sacred Scripture (see *CCC* 76). In addition, Jesus gave us the Magisterium to faithfully expound the priceless Deposit of Faith contained in Sacred Scripture and Sacred Tradition, again under the guidance of the Holy Spirit. We are so blessed to have such a perfect Bridegroom who thought of everything. As Vatican II teaches, these three divine gifts—Sacred Scripture, Sacred Tradition and the Magisterium—"are so linked and joined together that one cannot stand without the others, and that all together and each in its own way under the action of the one Holy Spirit contribute effectively to the salvation of souls" (*Dei Verbum*, number 10).

Let us pray:

Dear Father, Son and Holy Spirit, I want to fully embrace the gifts of Sacred Scripture, Sacred Tradition and the Magisterium's faithful exposition of the Deposit of Faith. I want to imitate Mary in her love and trust and become like Jesus in His total surrender to the will of the Father. Blessed Trinity, I want to be a light to a world steeped in darkness. Please honor my request to be a bearer of your light as I pray along with all the angels and saints:

Radiating Christ

~Venerable John Henry Cardinal Newman

Dear Jesus,

Help me to spread your fragrance wherever I go.

Flood my soul with your Spirit and Life.

Penetrate and possess my being so utterly

That my life may only be a radiance of Yours.

Shine through me, and be so in me

That every soul I come in contact with

May feel your Presence in my soul.

Let them look up, and see no longer me but only Jesus.

Stay with me,

And then I will begin to shine as You shine,

So to shine as to be a light to others.

The light, O Jesus, will be all from You.

None of it will be mine.

It will be You, shining on others through me.

Let me thus praise You

In the way in which You love best:

By shining on those around me.

Let me preach You without preaching,

Not by words but by example,

By the catching force,

The sympathetic influence of what I do,

The evident fullness of the love

My heart bears for You. Amen.

DAY THREE – Going Deeper with STMD

Now that you really understand the importance of this section of each chapter—is God calling you deeper? Following are ways to go deeper with Jesus, who calls you to see Him revealed in the Bible (Sacred Scripture), orthodox writings of the saints (faithful witness to Sacred Tradition) and the Catechism (Magisterium's faithful exposition of the Deposit of Faith)—STMD.

Jesus, I know You are the answer to all of my questions. Please reveal yourself to me in Sacred Scripture:

> *Always be prepared to make a defense to any one who calls you to account for the hope that is in you, yet do it with gentleness and reverence; and keep your conscience clear, so that, when you are abused, those who revile your good behavior in Christ may be put to shame. For it is better to suffer for doing right, if that should be God's will, than for doing wrong (1 Peter 3:15-17).*

> *But Mary kept all these things, pondering them in her heart (Luke 2:19).*

Memorize the above passages from Scripture, keep these things in your heart, and ponder them like Our Lady. What is God telling you here? Are you ready to give a gentle, reverent response when someone asks you about the reasons for your hope in Jesus Christ?

Feel free to find these passages in your Bible and read them in context. You may even want to read them once silently and then out loud. Spend some time thinking about them, and then take them to prayer. It is always a good idea to memorize verses of Sacred Scripture and make them your own. This is just another way to know Jesus (Who is the Eternal Word) a little better.

Jesus, I know You are the answer to all of my questions. Please reveal yourself to me in the orthodox writings of the saints, which provide a faithful witness to Sacred Tradition.

St. Augustine has this to say about belief (faith) and understanding reason), which is the very heart of STMD:

> "I believe, in order to understand; and I understand, the
> better to believe."

You might want to know more about the saint who is quoted above. A Weekday Missal is a great place to start when you want to know more about certain saints. And there are many good resources on the internet and in the library about great saints.

Jesus, I know You are the answer to all of my questions. Please reveal yourself to me in the Magisterium's faithful exposition of the Deposit of Faith.

The *Catechism of the Catholic Church* states:

One common source...

80 "Sacred Tradition and Sacred Scripture, then, are bound closely together and communicate one with the other. For both of them, flowing out from the same divine well-spring, come together in some fashion to form one thing and move towards the same goal." (*Dei Verbum* 9) Each of them makes present and fruitful in the Church the mystery of Christ, who promised to remain with his own "always, to the close of the age." (Mt 28:20)

You may want to read more about the topic of Sacred Scripture, Tradition and the Magisterium in the *Catechism,* by reviewing numbers 80-90 where the relationship between Tradition and Sacred Scripture is explained.

Use this space to write down any additional thoughts, prayers or epiphanies the Lord has given you during this teaching in your spiritual formation:

Chapter Ten

"How do I live centered in the Eucharist?"

P eople are asking, "How do I live a life centered in the
Eucharist?" The answer is: "Jesus." Let us begin now by
praying the "Our Father" along with Jesus, who gives Himself
to us in the Eucharist:

*In the name of the Father and of the Son and of the Holy
Spirit. Amen.*

*Our Father who art in heaven, hallowed be Thy Name. Thy
Kingdom come. Thy will be done, on earth as it is in heaven.
Give us this day our daily bread, and forgive us our trespasses,
as we forgive those who trespass against us, and lead us not into
temptation, but deliver us from evil. Amen.*

Our Lady of the Most Holy Trinity, pray for us.

*In the name of the Father and of the Son and of the Holy
Spirit. Amen.*

"How do I live a life centered in the Eucharist?" "Jesus is
the Eucharist."

Some people say, "Prove it to me. Prove the mystery of the

Eucharist to me." But remember, faith comes before understanding. The greatest minds in the history of the world believed in the Eucharist. Yet the Eucharist is not about scientific proofs, even though we have credible evidence that confirm so much of what the Church teaches. The all-powerful God, who created everything can thereby supersede the laws of nature. God manifests His power in the miracle of the Eucharist, suspending or transcending the laws of nature. Indeed, a miracle takes place at each authentic Catholic Mass as Jesus becomes really, truly and substantially present in the Most Holy Eucharist, *not only in our Mass but in Mass all around the world every day!* Are we going to tell God, "Lord, You must be subject to the laws of nature and science. You who created nature, and gave us science—you must be subject to those laws"? No, we're not. Or at least we shouldn't. Because Our God who created us and the whole universe knows what is best to do.

In the Most Holy Eucharist, Jesus gives us His Body, Blood, Soul and Divinity. Consider what it means to have a "soul relationship" with Jesus. The faculties of the soul include the memory, the intellect and the will. When we receive the Eucharist, we enter deeply into this "soul relationship" and we put on the mind and heart of Christ. We also receive the grace to live all the Gospels, all the teachings of Christ, and the whole Deposit of Faith (if we are open to this great gift of the Eucharist).

The great St. Augustine says, "If you have received worthily, you are what you have received." Think about that for a minute …. "If you have received worthily, you are what you have received." If you receive Jesus, you receive *all* of Jesus. Jesus does not give Himself in pieces. Jesus teaches us to give *all* of ourselves, and to be really present to other people. You know how it is when somebody is really present to you—it is beautiful. But, if the person we are talking to is mentally scattered, constantly looking at his or her watch, or looking all around, it is very awkward, and it hurts. Jesus is totally and completely present in the Most Holy Eucharist. He is really, truly, and substantially present: Body, Blood, Soul and Divinity. The smallest particle of the Eucharist is the whole Jesus. He gives us His whole self, and He teaches us to give all of ourselves. He teaches us in the Eucharist.

Perhaps the most difficult part of living the Eucharistic life (a life of thanksgiving) appears to us in the two greatest commandments. The greatest commandment is challenging as we are commanded to love God with our whole heart, mind, soul and strength. Yet, it is the second greatest commandment (love your neighbor as yourself for the love of God) where we really discover whether or not we are truly living the Eucharistic life.

For most of us, loving God is a deeply rooted premise of life. But the other "loves" of our lives, the ones that involve daily interaction on the merely human level, can seem more difficult. Sometimes being kind and attentive to the cashier at the grocery store is easier than being gentle toward our own spouse, children or siblings. We want to love as Jesus loves, but we are not exactly sure how to do this. Or, we are not really sure what "loving as Jesus loves" actually means.

John Paul II, in his letter to the bishops of the Church regarding the mystery and worship of the Eucharist (*Dominicae Cenae*), gives us some insight concerning how to become like Jesus in loving those around us:

"The authentic sense of the Eucharist becomes of itself the school of active love for neighbor. We know that this is the true and full order of love that the Lord has taught us: 'By this love you have for one another, everyone will know that you are my disciples.' The Eucharist educates us to this love in a deeper way; it shows us, in fact, what value each person, our brother or sister has in God's eyes, if Christ offers himself equally to each one, under the species of bread and wine. If our Eucharistic worship is authentic, it must make us grow in awareness of the dignity of each person. The awareness of that dignity becomes the deepest motive of our relationship with our neighbor."[30]

So let's consider this for a moment. John Paul II says that the Eucharist shows us what value each person has in God's eyes if Christ offers Himself equally to each one of us. We all have our opinions about other people, some favorable and some not so favorable. But we can grow in humility (and therefore in holiness) when we more fully understand this truth. If the Lord of the universe so values His children as to "offer himself equally to each one," what right do *we* have to pass judgment on a person?

This is a difficult teaching to accept and practice, so if you feel challenged, that is good, because you should be challenged to love others as Jesus has first loved you. In fact, this is the "new commandment" that Jesus gives us at the Last Supper: to love as He loves. At the Last Supper Jesus instituted the Holy Eucharist and the Priesthood of the New and Everlasting Covenant so that we could

. . . .

30 Pope John Paul II, *Dominicae Cenae*, No. 6.

live in His love. Jesus in the Eucharist does not call us to a "safe" love with boundaries—which isn't real love. Nor does He call us to a "conditional" love with limits—which also is not real love. Jesus Christ in the Eucharist calls us to a radical love—a love of total self-giving, even unto death.

Some may say that this is a "hard saying," just like those who were present at the Eucharistic discourse found in chapter 6 of St. John's Gospel. Jesus spoke the Truth that *"Unless you eat the flesh of the Son of man and drink His blood, you have no life in you"* (verse 53), and *"He who eats my flesh and drinks my blood has eternal life and I will raise him up on the last day"* (verse 54). Many found this to be a "hard saying" because they knew that Jesus was speaking literally. They knew that they would be cut off from Old Covenant Israel if they consumed any blood (Leviticus 17:14), and thus they knew they were being called to a radical trust that Jesus would deliver on his promises about life. Indeed, when Jesus says *"For my flesh is food indeed, and my blood is drink indeed"* (verse 55), He means it. And He is promising to feed us with Himself so we may abide in His love and fulfill all He commands.

Please prayerfully read all of the Eucharistic Discourse in chapter 6 of St. John's Gospel, and honestly reflect upon this gift of the Most Holy Eucharist. Realize that Jesus was speaking literally, for He did not run after those who left Him at this "hard saying." He did not chase after them to say, "Hey, guys, I was only speaking figuratively." Rather, *Jesus said to the twelve, "Do you also wish to go away?"* (verse 67). Jesus asks you the same question right now. Read verses 68 and 69 to see the response of St. Peter.

This way of total self-giving is what Jesus teaches, and He expects it from us as His disciples. "The Eucharist is above all else a sacrifice.... All who participate with faith in the Eucharist become aware that it is a 'sacrifice', that is to say a 'consecrated offering'.... The Church's intention is that the faithful not only offer the spotless victim [who is of course, Jesus], but also learn to offer themselves and daily be drawn into ever more perfect union, through Christ the Mediator, with the Father and with each other, so that at last God may be all in all."[31]

We all know that Jesus is the spotless victim who offers Himself for us, but the challenge is the reciprocal offering of ourselves to Him. A common theme in our discussion of the Eucharist is how *true* love (*Jesus'* love) makes demands. Real love entails sacrifice. But we don't need to fear this total gift of self, for we receive it in the Eucharist. Through the power of Jesus in the Eucharist, we find ourselves so given over to Christ and taken up by His love, that to do the Father's will is our only desire (as it was for Him). And this is the only way to really become like Jesus—to love doing the Father's will.

Our motives really matter here. If we do the Father's will, but not for love, then we have not reached our potential. But if we obey and serve because we have a heart overflowing with love for God, then we actualize our potential and grow in holiness. We need to love as Jesus loves and serve as He serves. And we can only do that through the graces that we receive in the Most Holy Eucharist, with the power of the Holy Spirit dwelling in us. When we love and trust the Father completely, we find that all things are possible with God because He

. . . .

31 Pope John Paul II, *Dominicae Cenae*, No. 9.
   Instituto Generalis Missalis Romani, 55f.: *Missale Romanum*, ed. cit., p. 40.

gives us His Beloved Son in the Sacraments. Thus, we can "learn to offer [ourselves] and daily be drawn into ever more perfect union, through Christ the Mediator, with the Father and with each other, so that at last God may be all in all" (John Paul II).

That is our ultimate goal in fulfilling the two greatest commandments—perfect love, therefore perfect communion. Remember, that communion begets communion. St. Maximilian Kolbe (the great martyr of charity) tells us that "The culmination of the Mass is not the consecration, but communion." And we remember St. Augustine saying, "If you have received worthily, you are what you have received." If we worthily receive Our Lord in the Eucharist, we will receive all that is necessary to fulfill the two greatest commandments (to love God and one another) and to live our vocation with zeal, joy and fidelity.

Blessed Mother Teresa of Calcutta said, "The time you spend with Jesus in the Blessed Sacrament is the best time you will spend on earth. Each moment you spend with Jesus will deepen your union with him, and make your soul everlastingly more glorious and beautiful in heaven."

If we want to become like Jesus, and grow in deeper union with Him, the Father, and the Holy Spirit, and if we want to promote unity among all people, then we should take certain steps. First, we need to become well-disposed to receive Our Lord in the Eucharist. To help in this process, consecrating ourselves to Jesus through Mary (see next chapter) is certainly recommended, as we learn how to prepare for Holy Communion, receive Holy Communion, and thank God for Holy Communion with Our Lady. We should also spend time in thanksgiving after Mass, and visit Jesus often where He patiently waits for us in the tabernacle. John Paul II tells us we must remember that "The Eucharist is a common possession of the whole Church as the Sacrament of her unity."[32] The more we put into preparation and reception of this sublime gift, the more we contribute to this Sacrament of unity. Our worthy reception of the Eucharist not only helps us grow in charity and holiness, but it benefits the whole Church.

His Holiness Pope Benedict XVI reminds us that "Worship pleasing to God can never be a purely private matter, without consequences for our relationships with others: it demands a public witness to our faith … there is nothing more beautiful than to be surprised by the Gospel, by the encounter with Christ. There is nothing more beautiful than to know him and to speak to others of our friendship with him."

A life centered in Jesus (who is the Eucharist) is a life lived for others. Jesus in the Eucharist gives us His very own Body, Blood, Soul and Divinity; and we are graced with the strength to love as He loves. Through the power of the Most Holy Eucharist, we can begin to "love our neighbor as we love ourselves." This Eucharistic life (this life of thanksgiving) is a life which sings the goodness of the Lord. It is a life that desires to share the rare beauty of the Banquet of the Lamb.

Pope Benedict continues, "The love that we celebrate in the sacrament is not something we can keep to ourselves. By its very nature it demands to be shared with all. What the world needs is God's love; it needs to encounter Christ and to believe in him. The

32 Pope John Paul II, *Dominicae Cenae*, No. 12.

Eucharist is thus the source and summit not only of the Church's life, but also of her mission: 'an authentically Eucharistic Church is a missionary Church.'"[33]

We begin to fulfill the two greatest commandments to love God above all things, and to love others as we love ourselves, when we share the Good News of the Eucharist (cf. *CCC* 2055, 1822). His Holiness further states, "The first and fundamental mission that we receive from the sacred mysteries we celebrate is that of bearing witness by our lives. The wonder we experience at the gift God has made to us in Christ gives new impulse to our lives and commits us to becoming witnesses of his love.... The more ardent the love for the Eucharist in the hearts of the Christian people, the more clearly will they recognize the goal of all mission: *to bring Christ to others.*"[34]

We cannot be convincing until we are fully convinced. May we all be fully convinced of the love of Christ in the Most Holy Sacrament of the Altar. "My Lord Jesus Christ, I firmly believe that I am about to receive, in Communion, Your Body, Your Blood, Your Soul and Your Divinity. I believe it because You have said it and I am ready to give my life to maintain this truth. Amen" (Communion Prayer).

Along with our Holy Father, let us "reflect on a notion dear to the early Christians, which also speaks eloquently to us today; namely, witness even to the offering of one's own life, to the point of martyrdom.... The Christian who offers his life in martyrdom enters

. . . .
33 Benedict XVI, *Sacramentum Caritatis*, No. 84.
34 Benedict XVI, *Sacramentum Caritatis*, No. 85 & 86.

into full communion with the Pasch of Jesus Christ and thus becomes Eucharist with Him. Today, too, the Church does not lack martyrs who offer the supreme witness to God's love. Even if the test of martyrdom is not asked of us, we know that worship pleasing to God demands that we should be inwardly prepared for it. Such worship culminates in the joyful and convincing testimony of a consistent Christian life, wherever the Lord calls us to be His witnesses."[35]

Jesus said, *"I am the living bread which came down from heaven; if anyone eats of this bread, he will live forever; and the bread which I shall give for the life of the world is my flesh" (John 6:51).* And from the depths of our hearts we reply, "Amen, Lord Jesus. We believe."

The faithful are renewed in the Eucharist every day through communion with the Most Holy Trinity. Jesus (as the High Priest) came to restore all of creation as an act of praise to the Most Holy Trinity. Indeed, your entire life is to become a hymn of praise to the Most Holy Trinity. Let us be moved to the Everlasting Life of God made present in the Eucharist. Come live the Eternal Life now, and experience the joy of Christ to the end of time! If you live in the Paschal Mystery of Christ in the Eucharist, you move from Sacrificial Death to Resurrection. A new birth takes place in your life when you receive the Eucharist. Jesus, by dying on the Cross says, "Sacrifice with me." The Eucharist is a sacrifice—the Eucharistic Sacrifice.

In the Eucharist we receive the secret of the Resurrection, the medicine of immortality. Do you want the medicine of immortality?

---

35 Pope Benedict XVI, *Sacramentum Caritatis*, No. 85.

The antidote to death is contained in the Eucharist. Do you want the antidote to death? We live right now in a culture of death. It is time for life to be made fully present, and that only takes place in the Eucharist. The Eucharist reinforces communion with heaven. It unites heaven and earth. We are united to the heavenly liturgy, and the vast array of holy Angels and saints that shout, *"Salvation belongs to our God who sits upon the throne, and to the Lamb!" (Rev. 7:10).* Do you want to be united to the heavenly liturgy? Do you want to sing the eternal praises of God with Our Lady and all of the Holy Angels and Saints? Then you want to live a life centered in the Eucharist.

DAY ONE – Imitating Mary – Woman of the Eucharist

Our Lady's "Fiat" & Our Own "Fiat"

We can accept this Eucharistic Way of Life as Our Lady said "Yes!" to it. She said "Yes!" to the plan of God as related to her through the Archangel Gabriel. She said "Yes!" to God at the foot of the Cross. She said "Yes!" to God and she became the Mother of the Church and thus the Mother of us all. She said "Yes!" to God and she became the Queen of heaven and earth. She helps us understand the Eucharistic Mystery of our lives. We find Our Lady reaffirming the Gospels and teaching us how to live the Eucharist, which gives us the strength to live the Gospels. She says, *"Do whatever He tells you" (John 2:5).* He tells us to eat His Flesh and drink His Blood. This is the manifestation of His love and mercy. We learn to say "Yes!" to God when we say "Yes!" to the Eucharist.

Let us come to Him in the Eucharist. Let us humble ourselves (like

Our Lady) to receive Our Lord and have the joy that Our Lady had at the Annunciation and the Incarnation. Let us not be so proud that we separate ourselves from the greatest gift that we can receive as a human person here on earth. In the Heart of Jesus in the Eucharist is the unity of God and man. We receive Him—Body, Blood, Soul and Divinity. Then we have a real, true, and substantial communion with God. The union of God and man occurs in Holy Communion. This is the marriage of mankind with God. Jesus is the Bridegroom and we are the Bride. God loves His Bride so much that He gives Himself totally to her. He died on the Cross for His Bride, so we could be cleansed and purified and presented holy, spotless, and undefiled—so we could live a holy way of life. The Eucharist is the gift of God to us. The Eucharist unites heaven and earth with an eternal embrace of oneness in Jesus. God created a perfect unity of mankind with Himself in the Person of Jesus Christ. Much like how the Blessed Virgin Mary was united to Jesus in her womb, we are united to Him in the Eucharist.

Together with Our Blessed Mother and the whole Church, we are to constantly turn our gaze "to [our] Lord, present in the Sacrament of the Altar," and "discover the full manifestation of his boundless love." How can we live a life of Eucharist (which means "thanksgiving") so as to reveal this boundless love and make it tangible to others?

DAY TWO – Becoming Like Jesus – Who Is the Eucharist

The Eucharist: A Call to Service

The Lord wishes to remain with you in the Eucharist. He desires communion with you. Communion is the answer to all of your problems. Be reconciled with God, with yourself, and with others. Remember how Jesus washed the feet of the Apostles at the Last Supper? This represents the need to serve. You draw the strength to serve in the Eucharist. In the Eucharist you are committed to changing the lives of those around you. This is the fruit of a transfigured existence. Jesus works in the hearts and minds of all who receive Him to bring the world into accordance with His Gospel. When you live centered in Jesus, Who is the Eucharist, you become a blessing to everyone.

In the Book of Revelation we read, *"The Spirit and the Bride say, 'Come…Come Lord, Jesus.'"* That is our cry as we approach Jesus in the Eucharist. Jesus in the Eucharist renews the Church, the family of God, in the power of the Holy Spirit. **When you approach Holy Communion, realize that God is taking you into Himself before you are taking Him into yourself. Everything starts with God and ends with God. This will change your life if you can grasp the reality that you are stepping right into God in Holy Communion.** God takes you into Himself first before you receive Him, so prepare well to enter into communion with Him, and He will change your life. You are stepping right into God. This is your life. You are called to a divine life, a profound life. You are called to the "Eucharistic Mystery" of your life.

Prayerfully consider your preparation for Holy Communion. Become more properly disposed to receive Jesus in the Eucharist this week. Here are some ideas to help you properly prepare to receive the manifold gifts Our Lord has in store for you:

- Receive the Sacrament of Penance and Reconciliation ("Confession")

- Arrive at the church early to pray before Mass

- Visit Our Lord in the tabernacle or participate in Eucharistic Adoration some time(s) during the week

- Prepare with Our Lady, receive with Our Lady, and thank God with Our Lady

- Spend time after receiving the Lord in joyful thanksgiving

- Make a prayer intention to live the Eucharist more fully by "loving your neighbor as you love yourself for the love of God."

- Look for ways to love as Jesus loves by giving yourself completely, and

- Follow John Paul II in his direction to the faithful:

"This way of total self-giving is what Jesus teaches us and it is what He expects of us as his disciples. The Eucharist is above all else a sacrifice....All who participate with faith in the Eucharist become aware that it is a 'sacrifice', that is to say a 'consecrated offering'.... The Church's intention is that the faithful not only offer the spotless victim [who is of course, Jesus], but also learn to offer themselves and daily be drawn into ever more perfect union, through Christ the Mediator, with the Father and with each other, so that at last God may be all in all."[36]

. . . .

36 Pope John Paul II, *Dominicae Cenae*, No. 9.
   Instituto Generalis Missalis Romani, 55f.: *Missale Romanum*, ed. cit., p. 40.

Let us pray:

Dear Father, Son and Holy Spirit, I want to live a life centered in the Most Holy Eucharist. I want the Eucharist to be the source of strength in my life. Help me to love Jesus in the Eucharist as Our Lady loved Him. Increase my Faith in the Real, True and Substantial Presence of Jesus in the Most Holy Eucharist and cause my devotion to Jesus in the Most Blessed Sacrament to grow and be strengthened each time I approach the Sacrament. Let the strength I find in the Eucharist inspire me and help me to be a blessing to all those around me. I ask all of this through the intercession of Mary, Mother of the Eucharist. In the Name of the Father and of the Son and of the Holy Spirit. Amen.

DAY THREE – Going Deeper with STMD

Is God calling you deeper? Following are ways to go deeper with Jesus, who calls you to see Him revealed in the Bible (Sacred Scripture), orthodox writings of the saints (faithful witness to Sacred Tradition) and the Catechism (Magisterium's faithful exposition of the Deposit of Faith)—STMD.

Jesus, I know You are the answer to all of my questions. Please reveal yourself to me in Sacred Scripture:

> Jesus said, *"I am the living bread which came down from heaven; if anyone eats of this bread, he will live forever; and the bread which I shall give for the life of the world is my flesh"* (John 6:51).

Feel free to find this passage in your Bible and read it in context.

Every Catholic Christian should be familiar with chapter 6 of the Gospel of John. It is a good message to share with Protestants who have not yet awakened to the gift of Jesus in the Eucharist. You should read this chapter of John once silently, then out loud, then spend some time thinking about it, and take it to prayer. It is always a good idea to memorize verses of Sacred Scripture and make them your own. This is just another way to know Jesus (Who is the Eternal Word) a little better.

Jesus, I know You are the answer to all of my questions. Please reveal yourself to me in the orthodox writings of the saints, which provide a faithful witness to Sacred Tradition.

Here is what St. Cyril of Alexandria has to say about the Most Holy Eucharist:

> "As two pieces of wax fused together make one, so he
> who receives Holy Communion is so united with Christ
> that Christ is in him and he is in Christ."

Ask yourself, "What does it mean to be 'fused together' and 'made one' with Christ who is the Lord of the Universe?"

You might want to know more about the saint who is quoted above. A Weekday Missal is a great place to start when you want to know more about certain saints. And there are many good resources on the internet and in the library about great saints.

Jesus, I know You are the answer to all of my questions. Please reveal yourself to me in the Magisterium's faithful exposition of the Deposit of Faith.

You can turn to the *Catechism of the Catholic Church,*

number 1324:

> The Eucharist is "the source and summit of the Christian
> life." (*Lumen gentium* 11) "The other sacraments,
> and indeed all ecclesiastical ministries and works of
> the apostolate, are bound up with the Eucharist and
> are oriented toward it. For in the blessed Eucharist is
> contained the whole spiritual good of the Church, namely
> Christ himself, our Pasch." (*Presbyterorum ordinis* 5)

You may wish to read the *Catechism* beginning with number 1322
and continuing until number 1419 in order to gain an even deeper
knowledge and appreciation of the Most Holy Sacrament of the Altar.

Use this space to write down any additional thoughts, prayers
or epiphanies the Lord has given you during this teaching in your
spiritual formation:

Chapter Eleven

"How do I live True Devotion?"

People are asking, "How do I live True Devotion?" The answer is: "Jesus." Let us begin now by praying the "Our Father" along with Jesus, Who is the ultimate goal of our True Devotion:

In the name of the Father and of the Son and of the Holy Spirit. Amen.

Our Father who art in heaven, hallowed be Thy Name. Thy Kingdom come. Thy will be done, on earth as it is in heaven. Give us this day our daily bread, and forgive us our trespasses, as we forgive those who trespass against us, and lead us not into temptation, but deliver us from evil. Amen.

Our Lady of the Most Holy Trinity, pray for us.

In the name of the Father and of the Son and of the Holy Spirit. Amen.

The nature of perfect devotion to the Blessed Virgin Mary is perfect consecration to Jesus Christ. If you follow the call to Consecration to Jesus in Mary, your life will be blessed abundantly.

If you become consecrated to Jesus in Mary, your life will never be the same. Our Lady promises those who are consecrated through her to Jesus that she will oversee all of their affairs, so they are free to take care of hers. What a wonderful exchange—Our Blessed Mother, who is Queen of heaven and earth (the Mother of God by God's own choice), will oversee all our affairs as a mother, with love and care and tender affection. She does this for us to free us from all our worries, anxieties, and cares (the things that distract us from fulfilling the Plan of God). She will care for our loved ones and everything else so that we can serve God's will under her mantle of protection.

What is standing in the way of your path to holiness? That is the primary question that St. Louis Marie de Montfort (a devoted son of Our Blessed Mother, and the author of *True Devotion*) wants us to consider as we begin this preparation. Satan put many obstacles and snares in the path of St. Louis Marie de Montfort when he wrote *True Devotion*. Even after its completion, the original manuscript was hidden during the French Revolution, and was found many years later by a Montfort Father. Satan knows that those souls who are consecrated to Jesus through Mary (and are living out that consecration daily) are lost to him forever. So expect some challenges along this path into Our Lady's Heart. And know that your actual consecration will be blessed and worthwhile.

The preparation for Consecration takes place over a 33-day period. The first part of the preparation takes twelve days and focuses on "cleaning your spiritual house," or what de Montfort calls, "Ridding Oneself of the Spirit of the World." The three other sections are "Knowledge of Self," "Knowledge of Our Lady" and "Knowledge of

Christ," which take seven days each.

In the first twelve days, St. Louis Marie de Montfort says you need to:

> Examine your conscience, pray, practice renouncement of
> your own will; mortification, purity of heart. This purity
> is the indispensable condition for contemplating God in
> heaven, to see Him on earth and to know Him by the light
> of faith.[37]

In short, St. Louis is asking you to remove the spirit of the world. The way of the world and the way of Christ are simply not compatible. This may seem obvious, but sometimes it is not so clear. Sometimes we do things our own way, and still call ourselves disciples of Christ. Sometimes we don't realize how self-centered we have become until we take the time to reflect. This interior reflection is the focus of the first twelve days. You are invited to examine your life and ask the very tough questions:

- What is standing in the way of my path to holiness?

- How have I allowed the spirit of the world to reign in my life?

The spirit of the world is anything that is contrary to the Spirit of Jesus Christ. Our Lord will never share a throne, so any false idol in your life needs to be exposed and overthrown.

Wherever we have made ourselves sovereign, we have put an obstacle in our path to holiness. Whenever we decide that we know

---

37 *Preparation for Total Consecration According to St. Louis Marie de Montfort*, pg. 1.

better than Holy Mother Church, we put an obstacle in our path to holiness. Whenever we choose to take matters into our own hands instead of relying on God's Providence, we put an obstacle in our path to holiness.

Our loving God, through St. Louis Marie de Montfort, is giving us an incredible gift in these first twelve days. He is giving us the opportunity to identify and remove these obstacles in our path. He is helping us to clear the way and make straight the path to Jesus, so that we can serve Him fully, completely, and without reserve.

Make a resolution to embrace this time of prayerful reflection. Ask the Blessed Trinity to reveal any obstacles you may have placed in the path, and then beg for their removal and annihilation. If you are sincere, then in twelve days you will have gained much insight and renounced the spirit of the world. You will have committed yourself to let Our Lady and the Holy Spirit lead you closer to God. Then you will be making long strides along the path to holiness.

The next seven days of the preparation will take you through knowledge of self. Although this can be a daunting subject for most people, the Word has some encouragement for you here. Jesus says, *"And I tell you, Ask, and it will be given you; seek, and you will find; knock, and it will be opened to you. For every one who asks receives, and he who seeks finds, and to him who knocks it will be opened"* (Luke 11:9-10). Claim the powerful words of Our Lord and set out boldly to continue your journey toward *Total Consecration to Jesus through Mary,* according to the method of St. Louis Marie de Montfort.

In order to clearly see flaws within ourselves, we usually need someone to speak the truth to us. Mary's whole life was and is centered in Christ, Who is Truth and Love. So Our Blessed Mother can "speak the truth to us in love." If God the Father entrusted His only Son to her, we should also entrust ourselves to her. The following words of St. Louis Marie de Montfort describe the role of Mary in our knowledge of self.

"Prayers, examens, reflection, acts of renouncement of our own will, of contrition for our sins, of contempt of self, ALL PERFORMED AT THE FEET OF MARY, for it is from her that we hope for light to know ourselves. It is near her, that we shall be able to measure the abyss of our miseries without despairing."[38]

When we begin to see ourselves in the light of Christ, we need to be prepared for what we might see. Some of us have problems being honest with ourselves about our selfishness or sinfulness. Some of us have areas of pride that we have not yet renounced. And some of us have areas of addictions or poor habits of various sorts. Whatever is the obstacle, we need to realize how it is wounding us and how it is preventing us from living fully in Jesus Christ. This will all be so much easier if we do it in the company of Mary.

Hear these words spoken to you from the cross by Our Lord and Savior Jesus Christ:

> *When Jesus saw his mother, and the disciple whom he loved standing near, he said to his mother, "Woman, behold, your son!" Then he said to the disciple, "Behold,*

. . . .

38 *Preparation for Total Consecration According to St. Louis Marie de Montfort,* pg. 21 [emphasis added].

your mother!" And from that hour the disciple took her to his own home (John 19:26-27).

Ask yourself:

- Have you made enough room for Our Lady in your life?

- Have you "taken her into your home"?

During this seven-day portion of the preparation, we pray that you will have the courage to ask Mary for light to know yourself fully, even as you are fully known:

> *"And I tell you, Ask, and it will be given you; seek, and you will find; knock, and it will be opened to you. For every one who asks receives, and he who seeks finds, and to him who knocks it will be opened" (Luke 11:9-10).*

John Paul II said of *True Devotion*:

> "The reading of this book was a decisive turning-point in my life. I say 'turning-point' but in fact it was a long inner journey…. This 'perfect devotion' is indispensable to anyone who means to give himself without reserve to Christ and to the work of redemption. It is from Montfort that I have taken my motto: *Totus tuus*' ('I am all thine'). Someday I'll have to tell you Montfortians how I discovered de Montfort's *Treatise on True Devotion to Mary*, and how often I had to reread it to understand it."

Ask yourself:
- Where am I on the path to holiness?

- What does it mean to "give [myself] without reserve to Christ and to the work of redemption"?

- How can I embrace the motto of John Paul II and truly say to Our Lord and Our Lady, "Totus, tuus ... I am ALL thine"?"

Remember these words of St. Louis Marie de Montfort and make them your own:

"The more we honor the Blessed Virgin, the more we honor Jesus Christ, because we honor Mary only that we may the more perfectly honor Jesus, since we go to her only as the way by which we are to find the end we are seeking, which is JESUS."

Resources

Before we continue with True Devotion, we wish to share a few resources that will help your consecration go more smoothly. First, we suggest you read the book, *True Devotion* by St. Louis Marie de Montfort. It is from this book that *Total Consecration to Jesus through Mary* is derived. We also recommend a booklet which includes all of the prayers and readings for the 33-day preparation period. You may purchase the book (*True Devotion*) and/or the preparation booklet (*Preparation for Total Consecration to Jesus through Mary*) from the Montfort Fathers at the Montfort Publications website www.publications.montfortmissionaries.org/catalog. You may also download the consecration prayers/readings (free) from the www.Fisheaters.com website.

DAY ONE – Imitating Mary through True Devotion

Knowledge of Mary

The next seven-day portion of *Preparation for Total Consecration to Jesus Living in Mary* focuses on the knowledge of Mary. Remember that True Devotion to Mary began with Jesus. There is only one True Devotion. And St. Louis tells us that there are many false devotions as well. Both of these can be expressed through the following meditations:

Imagine Our Lady (radiant and beautiful) standing at your front door. She gently knocks upon your door, and now everything is up to you. As you move toward the door, you must decide how to receive her. How will you interact with her after opening the door? Will you joyfully embrace her and lean on her maternal heart with the affection of an only child? Will you simply shake her hand as she enters, showing her respect, but lacking in any real affection? Will you incline your head politely, but refuse to extend your hand to her, somehow thinking that it would show too much reverence? Or will you pretend that you are not at home, and leave her standing outside the door? How will you treat the Queen of All Hearts when she comes to your front door? What will you do?

The True Devotee is easy to recognize here, and so are the false devotees. Ask yourself truthfully, which one am I? If you don't like your answer, now ask yourself, which one do I hope to become?

While Our Lady is in heaven and doesn't experience love the same way we do, her love is actually more intense. Our Lady wants you to know that you are her beloved child, and that you are precious to her. Our Lord made her Our Mother as He hung on the Cross for us, and she lovingly accepted this relationship with all of us, and placed us all in the very center of Her Immaculate Heart. Is there any other way to respond to love, other than love? Can you imagine her sadness from those who ignore her? And many people revile her and speak evil of her.

Still others see her and acknowledge her, yet when she comes toward them with open arms, they only nod politely, not returning any love to her. Think of how it feels to passionately express your love for someone, only to have your love rejected. She faces that every day. The *least* we can do is return love for love. Your Mother deeply and sincerely loves you. Talk to her today. Speak about your relationship, and no matter how it has been in the past (whether good or bad) resolve to improve it together. Let her take you by the hand. You will always be happy that you did.

"We must unite ourselves to Jesus through Mary—this is the characteristic of our devotion; therefore St. Louis de Montfort asks that we employ ourselves in acquiring a knowledge of the Blessed Virgin." (Part III—Knowledge of Mary)

Ask yourself:

• How will I get to know my Blessed Mother even better this week?

• How can I serve her?

• How can I love her as she deserves to be loved?

DAY TWO – Becoming Like Jesus through True Devotion

Knowledge of Jesus Christ

St. Louis Marie de Montfort teaches us in *True Devotion* that:

"Jesus Christ our Savior, true God and true Man, ought to be the last end of all our devotions, else they are false and delusive. Jesus Christ is the Alpha and the Omega, the beginning and the end of all things…. If then we establish solid devotion to Our Blessed Lady, it is only to establish more perfectly devotion to Jesus Christ, and to provide an easy and secure means for finding Jesus Christ. Devotion to Our Lady is necessary for us, as I have already shown, and will show still further hereafter, as a means of finding Jesus Christ perfectly, of loving Him tenderly, of serving Him faithfully."[39]

If you really want to know someone better, you should talk with his mother! There are things that only a mother knows about her child. The *Catechism* teaches us that "'God sent forth his Son,' but to prepare a body for him, (Gal 4:4; Heb 10:5) he wanted the free cooperation of a creature. For this, from all eternity God chose for the mother of his Son a daughter of Israel, a young Jewish woman of Nazareth in Galilee, 'a virgin betrothed to a man whose name was Joseph, of the house of David; and the virgin's name was Mary.' (Lk 1:26-27)"[40]

Mary is the one woman (in all of time and eternity) through which God chose to enter the human race. The Church calls the special honor we give her hyperdulia, which is a Greek word for the exalted

39 St. Louis Marie de Montfort, *True Devotion*, Nos. 61 & 62.
40 *Catechism of the Catholic Church*, 488.

reverence we give the Blessed Virgin Mary. We do not worship Mary. Rather, we hold her in a special place of honor since she is the Mother of God. Jesus honored his Mother, and so do we. It's really that simple.

We are treating the subject of knowledge of Jesus Christ, yet we continue to write about Mary. Why? Because the two of them *cannot* be separated—something that St. Louis Marie de Montfort discerned long ago. Without Mary, God does not cease to be God. However, Jesus Christ, in His perfect Wisdom, chose to take His human Flesh from Mary. So by *His* will, *His* plan, *His* purpose, and *His* design, the two are inseparably united throughout all eternity. But what does it mean to be eternally united? How can we understand this?

By now we understand that God has a plan for each of our lives, which was determined before the beginning of time at the "Council of the Most Holy Trinity." A purpose, plan, and mission was designed for each of us to either embrace or reject—each according to his own free will. The same is true of Mary.

The Most Holy Trinity (before all time began) chose Mary to be the Mother of God. The Father chose to have the Son make His dwelling among us in the Immaculate womb of a Virgin by the power of the Holy Spirit. And thus, *The Word became flesh and dwelt among us ... (John 1:14).*

So now we come to Him. We come to He Who Is. We come to the One with the Name above all other names. We come to Jesus, which means "God saves." At the Annunciation, the angel Gabriel revealed "Jesus" as His proper name, which expresses all-at-once His identity, purpose and mission (cf. *CCC* 430). Then at the Incarnation, with the full cooperation and consent of Our Blessed Mother, "Jesus united himself to all men" (*CCC* 432) and thus our hope of redemption became more than hope—it became a Divine reality.

So we now trace our redemption from the "Council of the Most Holy Trinity," and we travel through salvation history (from the Patriarchs and Prophets to the time of the Annunciation and the Incarnation) to the entire Paschal Mystery of Our Lord. When we view the eternal picture, we can begin to understand that once united, Our Lady and Our Lord *cannot* be separated. Those who have understood this mystery (like our dear St. Louis Marie de Montfort) have prayed and written much to aid us in our understanding. So we need to think this over for a while to more fully grasp it and make it our own, for it really is an amazing truth. God planned all things for our good from the beginning of time—what an awesome God!

St. Louis teaches us the beautiful effects of living out a total consecration to Our Lord through the Blessed Virgin, "By this practice, faithfully observed, you will give Jesus more glory in a month, than by any other practice, however difficult, in many years."[41]

Certainly, we all want to glorify Jesus with our lives. So it is very good that we are walking this road to "holy slavery" (as Montfort calls it) to Our Lady and Our Lord. Many people balk at the term "holy slavery," for slavery suggests that we no longer retain our rights and we are obliged to do the will of our master. These seem like radical and counter-cultural ideas, but in our Baptism we renounce Satan and the world, and we take Jesus Christ as our Savior and Lord. So

---

41 St. Louis Marie de Montfort, *True Devotion*, No. 225.

He is indeed our Master. The hard truth is that we are all creatures, and so we are all slaves, but we are allowed to choose whose slave we will be. We have two choices: Satan and sin or Jesus and freedom. Unholy slavery is self-imposed because we do have a choice to be free. Nevertheless, we *must* all choose one or the other.

St. Paul's letter to the Romans states:

> *Do you not know that if you yield yourselves to any one as obedient slaves, you are slaves of the one whom you obey, either of sin, which leads to death, or of obedience, which leads to righteousness? But thanks be to God, that you who were once slaves of sin have become obedient from the heart to the standard of teaching to which you were committed, and, having been set free from sin, have become slaves of righteousness. I am speaking in human terms, because of your natural limitations. For just as you once yielded your members to impurity and to greater and greater iniquity, so now yield your members to righteousness for sanctification. When you were slaves of sin, you were free in regard to righteousness. But then what return did you get from the things of which you are now ashamed? The end of those things is death. But now that you have been set free from sin and have become slaves of God, the return you get is sanctification and its end, eternal life. For the wages of sin is death, but the free gift of God is eternal life in Christ Jesus our Lord (Romans 6:16-23).*

Through the voices of the world, Satan deceives us by suggesting that we don't really need to choose, but that is a lie. Not only do we need to choose, but we are wise to fortify that choice through this Total Consecration to Our Lord through the Blessed Virgin Mary.

As a true disciple of Our Lord, always covered in the prayers and intercessions of Our Lady, and equipped by Our gracious Lord with "every spiritual blessing in the heavens," you now hear the words of the Great Commission spoken directly to you:

> *"All authority in heaven and on earth has been given to me. Go therefore and make disciples of all nations, baptizing them in the name of the Father and of the Son and of the Holy Spirit, teaching them to observe all that I have commanded you; and lo, I am with you always, to the close of the age" (Matthew 28: 18-20).*

So now go forward with the missionary mandate (under the mantle of Our Mother) to share this gift of Truth. Like Mary, let us remember that the Holy Spirit is "the origin and source of our sanctification" and invoke his assistance regularly (*CCC* 190, 2671). And let us "Make Mary the model for all [our] striving for perfection in holiness and virtues".[42] Living this Total Consecration each day will guide your quest to *Imitate Mary, Become Like Jesus and Live for the Triune God!*

May Almighty God bless you, the Father and the Son and the Holy Spirit. Amen.

. . . .

42 Rules of the Spiritual Life of the Society of Our Lady of the Most Holy Trinity, pg. 16, Rule 157.

Let us pray:

Dear Father, Son, and Holy Spirit, help me to love Mary even more than I do today. Show me how to trust her and to truly see myself as her beloved child. Help me to depend on her intercession and her help, just as a little child depends on his mother for everything. Thank you for the gift of Mary to me and to all of the human race. In the Name of the Father and of the Son and of the Holy Spirit. Amen.

DAY THREE – Going Deeper with STMD

Is God calling you deeper? Following are ways to go deeper with Jesus, who calls you to see Him revealed in the Bible (Sacred Scripture), orthodox writings of the saints (faithful witness to Sacred Tradition) and the Catechism (Magisterium's faithful exposition of the Deposit of Faith)—STMD.

Jesus, I know You are the answer to all of my questions. Please reveal yourself to me in Sacred Scripture:

> *"If any man would come after me, let him deny himself and take up his cross and follow me" (Mark 8:34).*

> *When Jesus saw his Mother, and the disciple whom he loved standing near, he said to his mother, "Woman, behold, your son!" Then he said to the disciple, "Behold, your mother!" And from that hour the disciple took her to his own home (John 19:26-27).*

Memorize the above passages from Scripture, and ponder them in your heart with Our Lady. What is God telling you here? These scriptural passages summarize the call to holiness. Ask His Majesty and Our Lady to give you the strength to live this Gospel message.

Jesus, I know You are the answer to all of my questions. Please reveal yourself to me in the orthodox writings of the saints, which provide a faithful witness to Sacred Tradition.

St. Louis Marie de Montfort has this to say about *True Devotion*:

"The more we honor the Blessed Virgin, the more we honor Jesus Christ, because we honor Mary only that we may the more perfectly honor Jesus, since we go to her only as the way by which we are to find the end we are seeking, which is Jesus."

You might want to know more about the saint who is quoted above. A Weekday Missal is a great place to start when you want to know more about certain saints. And there are many good resources on the internet and in the library about great saints.

Jesus, I know You are the answer to all of my questions. Please reveal yourself to me in the Magisterium's faithful exposition of the Deposit of Faith.

You can turn to the *Catechism of the Catholic Church*, number 488:

> "God sent forth his Son," but to prepare a body for him,
> (Gal 4:4; Heb 10:5) he wanted the free cooperation of
> a creature. For this, from all eternity God chose for the
> mother of his Son a daughter of Israel, a young Jewish
> woman of Nazareth in Galilee, "a virgin betrothed to a
> man whose name was Joseph, of the house of David; and
> the virgin's name was Mary." (Lk 1:26-27)

Enjoy a holy hour reading and meditating upon this passage. Ask the Blessed Trinity to reveal to you the truth of this counsel and its meaning for your life, vocation, and mission. Taking the time to meditate on this passage and asking the Trinity to "seal the graces" from this formation is a tremendous gift to yourself. Come, Holy Spirit, teach me how to live the Gospel!

Pray these words of great wisdom which came through the pen of St. Louis Marie de Montfort:

Tear away, noble soul,
Everything that's useless,
Force yourself to be adorned
With sovereign good alone.

Flee from the world and its splendor,
Enter deep in your own heart;
May it be your oratory,
Your distinction, your joy.

Flee disastrous luxury,
But maintain cleanliness.
Be humble and modest
With no affectation.

Make certain your family
Is your principal duty,
Form it with Gospel laws
And tolerate no evil.

Always give it the example

Of all sorts of good works

So the family deems you

Its mirror of Christian.

Use the space below to write down any additional thoughts, prayers or epiphanies the Lord has given you during this teaching in your spiritual formation:

"What now?"

Congratulations on your completion of this personal formation program, *Fiat!* We pray that you have received a time of deep prayer, reflection, and growth in your relationship with God (deepening your love of God, neighbor and self). You are a unique, precious, and unrepeatable human being with special talents and gifts. Our prayers continue for you as you continue on your personal journey of faith.

God wants you to share the wonderful love and freedom that you have found in Jesus Christ, with the people He has placed in your life. We encourage you to be a light to the world! Share Our Lady's way of life and the gift of formation that you have received with those you know and love. You may desire to join a community for ongoing formation, or you may be moved to start a small group study in your parish. We invite you to contact us at SOLT, to make arrangements for any further activity.

You can offer these formation materials to others by sharing our website (www.OurLadyLovesYou.org) or by giving them this book.

There are many people waiting for an opportunity to know, love, and serve God better, so they can be happy with Him forever in heaven. We receive much joy by helping someone else come to know and love God, and there is no better way to thank God for the gifts that you have been given than by sharing His love with others.

Remember, you are a unique, precious, unrepeatable human being, made in the image and likeness of God, and you are loved by the Father. He has a plan for your life, and He has work in His Kingdom for you that no one else can do. People are asking, "What now?" Let us take our direction from Our Lord Himself:

> *"All authority in heaven and on earth has been given to me. Go therefore and make disciples of all nations, baptizing them in the name of the Father and of the Son and of the Holy Spirit, teaching them to observe all that I have commanded you; and lo, I am with you always, to the close of the age" (Matthew 28: 18-20).*

Through the intercession of Our Lady, St. Joseph, St. Michael, St. Peter, St. Paul, St. John, St. James, St. Thérèse, St. Rita, St. Louis Marie de Montfort, St. Philomena, St. Jude, St. Nicholas, St. Alphonsus, St. Peter Chrysologus, St. Zachary, St. Elizabeth, St. John the Baptist, St. Perpetua, St. Felicity, St. Francis, St. Veronica Guiliani, St. Joan of Arc, St. Louis, St. Joseph Calasanz, St. Charles Borromeo, St. Padre Pio, St. Patrick, St. Bridget, St. Columban and all the Holy Angels and Saints, may you be abundantly blessed in the Covenant of Communion of the Most Holy Trinity—with my Priestly blessing, Father Zachary of the Mother of God, SOLT.

Imitate Mary, Become Like Jesus, Live for the Triune God

JMJ + OBT

Our Father

In the name of the Father and of the Son and of the Holy Spirit. Amen.

Our Father who art in heaven, hallowed be Thy Name. Thy Kingdom come. Thy will be done, on earth as it is in heaven. Give us this day our daily bread, and forgive us our trespasses, as we forgive those who trespass against us, and lead us not into temptation, but deliver us from evil. Amen

Our Lady of the Most Holy Trinity, pray for us.

In the name of the Father and of the Son and of the Holy Spirit. Amen.

Litany of the Blessed Virgin Mary (Litany of Loreto)

Lord, *have mercy on us.* Christ, *have mercy on us.* Lord, *have mercy on us.* Christ, *hear us.* Christ, *graciously hear us.*

God the Father of heaven, *have mercy on us.*
God the Son, Redeemer of the world, *have mercy on us.*

God the Holy Ghost, *have mercy on us.*

Holy Trinity, one God, *have mercy on us.*

Holy Mary, *pray for us.*

Holy Mother of God, *pray for us.*

Holy Virgin of virgins, *pray for us.*

Mother of Christ, *pray for us.*

Mother of divine grace, *pray for us.*

Mother most pure, *pray for us.*

Mother most chaste, *pray for us.*

Mother inviolate, *pray for us.*

Mother undefiled, *pray for us.*

Mother most amiable, *pray for us.*

Mother most admirable, *pray for us.*

Mother of good counsel, *pray for us.*

Mother of our Creator, *pray for us.*

Mother of our Savior, *pray for us.*

Virgin most prudent, *pray for us.*

Virgin most venerable, *pray for us.*

Virgin most renowned, *pray for us.*

Virgin most powerful, *pray for us.*

Virgin most merciful, *pray for us.*

Virgin most faithful, *pray for us.*

Mirror of justice, *pray for us.*

Seat of wisdom, *pray for us.*

Cause of our joy, *pray for us.*

Spiritual vessel, *pray for us.*

Vessel of honor, *pray for us.*

Singular vessel of devotion, *pray for us.*

Mystical rose, *pray for us.*

Tower of David, *pray for us.*

Tower of ivory, *pray for us.*

House of gold, *pray for us.*

Ark of the covenant, *pray for us.*

Gate of heaven, *pray for us.*

Morning star, *pray for us.*

Health of the sick, *pray for us.*

Refuge of sinners, *pray for us.*

Comforter of the afflicted, *pray for us.*

Help of Christians, *pray for us.*

Queen of Angels, *pray for us.*

Queen of Patriarchs, *pray for us.*

Queen of Prophets, *pray for us.*

Queen of Apostles, *pray for us.*

Queen of Martyrs, *pray for us.*

Queen of Confessors, *pray for us.*

Queen of Virgins, *pray for us.*

Queen of all Saints, *pray for us.*

Queen conceived without original sin, *pray for us.*

Queen assumed into heaven, *pray for us.*

Queen of the most holy Rosary, *pray for us.*

Queen of the family, *pray for us.*

Queen of Peace, *pray for us.*

Lamb of God, who takest away the sins of the world, *spare us, O Lord.*

Lamb of God, who takest away the sins of the world,

   graciously hear us, O Lord.

Lamb of God, who takest away the sins of the world, *have mercy on us.*

Pray for us, O holy Mother of God,

   that we may be made worthy of the promises of Christ.

Let us pray.

Grant, we beseech Thee, O Lord God, unto us Thy servants, that we may rejoice in continual health of mind and body; and, by the glorious intercession of the Blessed Mary ever Virgin, may be delivered from present sadness, and enter into the joy of Thine eternal gladness. Through Christ Our Lord. Amen.

Magnificat

from the Divine Office

My soul proclaims the greatness of the Lord, my spirit rejoices in God my Savior for He has looked with favor on His lowly servant. From this day all generations will call me blessed: the Almighty has done great things for me, and Holy is His Name. He has mercy on those who fear Him in every generation. He has shown the strength of His arm, He has scattered the proud in their conceit. He has cast down the mighty from their thrones, and has lifted up the lowly. He has filled the hungry with good things, and the rich He has sent away empty. He has come to the help of His servant Israel for He has remembered His promise of mercy, the promise He made to our fathers, to Abraham and his children forever (Luke 1:46-55).

Litany of the Holy Ghost

Lord, *have mercy on us.* Christ, *have mercy on us.* Lord, *have mercy on us.*

Father, all-powerful, *have mercy on us.*

Jesus, Eternal Son of the Father, Redeemer of the world, *save us.*

Spirit of the Father and the Son, boundless life of both, *sanctify us.*

Holy Ghost, who proceedest from the Father and the Son,
enter our hearts.

Holy Ghost, who are equal to the Father and the Son,
enter our hearts.

Promise of God the Father, *have mercy on us.*

Ray of heavenly light, *have mercy on us.*

Author of all good, *have mercy on us.*

Source of heavenly water, *have mercy on us.*

Consuming fire, *have mercy on us.*

Ardent charity, *have mercy on us.*

Spiritual unction, *have mercy on us.*

Spirit of love and truth, *have mercy on us.*

Spirit of wisdom and understanding, *have mercy on us.*

Spirit of counsel and fortitude, *have mercy on us.*

Spirit of knowledge and piety, *have mercy on us.*

Spirit of the fear of the Lord, *have mercy on us.*

Spirit of grace and prayer, *have mercy on us.*

Spirit of peace and meekness, *have mercy on us.*

Spirit of modesty and innocence, *have mercy on us.*

Holy Ghost the Comforter, *have mercy on us.*

Holy Ghost, the Sanctifier, *have mercy on us.*

Holy Ghost, Who governest the Church, *have mercy on us.*

Gift of God the Most high, *have mercy on us.*

Spirit who fillest the universe, *have mercy on us.*

Spirit of the adoption of the children of God, *have mercy on us.*

Holy Ghost, *inspire us with horror of sin.*

Holy Ghost, *come and renew the face of the earth.*

Holy Ghost, *engrave Thy law in our hearts.*

Holy Ghost, *inflame us with the flame of thy love.*

Holy Ghost, *open to us the treasures of Thy graces.*

Holy Ghost, *teach us to pray well.*

Holy Ghost, *enlighten us with Thy heavenly inspirations.*

Holy Ghost, *lead us in the way of salvation.*

Holy Ghost, *grant us the only necessary knowledge.*

Holy Ghost, *inspire in us the practice of good.*

Holy Ghost, *grant us the merits of all virtues.*

Holy Ghost, *make us persevere in justice.*

Holy Ghost, *be Thou our everlasting reward.*

Lamb of God, Who takest away the sins of the world,
   send us Thy Holy Ghost.

Lamb of God, Who takest away the sins of the world,
   pour down into our souls the gifts of the Holy Ghost.

Lamb of God, Who takest away the sins of the world,
   grant us the Spirit of wisdom and piety.

Come Holy Ghost, fill the hearts of Thy faithful.
   And enkindle in them the fire of Thy love.

Let us pray.

Grant, O merciful Father, that Thy Divine Spirit enlighten, inflame, and purify us, that He may penetrate us with His heavenly dew and make us fruitful in good works; through Our Lord Jesus Christ, Thy Son, Who with Thee, in the unity of the Holy Spirit, liveth and reigneth forever and ever. Amen.

Memorare

Remember, O most gracious Virgin Mary, that never was it known that anyone who fled to thy protection, implored thy help or sought thy intercession was left unaided. Inspired by this confidence, we fly unto thee, O Virgin of virgins, our Mother. To thee do we come, before thee we stand, sinful and sorrowful. O Mother of the Word incarnate, despise not our petitions, but in thy mercy hear and answer us. Amen.

St. Michael the Archangel

St. Michael the Archangel, defend us in battle. Be our protection against the wickedness and snares of the devil. May God rebuke him we humbly pray. And do Thou, O Prince of the heavenly hosts, by the power of God, cast into hell, Satan and all the other evil spirits who prowl about the world seeking the ruin of souls. Amen.

O Jesus Living in Mary

O Jesus living in Mary, come and live in Thy servants,

In the spirit of Thy holiness, in the fullness of Thy might,

In the truth of Thy virtues, in the perfection of Thy ways,

In the communion of Thy mysteries, subdue every hostile power

In Thy spirit, for the glory of the Father. Amen.

Ave Maris Stella

Hail, bright Star of Ocean, God's own Mother blest.

Ever sinless Virgin, Gate of Heavenly Rest.

Taking that sweet Ave, which from Gabriel came,

peace confirm within us, changing Eva's name.

Break the captive's fetters, light on blindness pour.

All our ills expelling, every bliss implore.

Show thyself a Mother, may the Word Divine,

born for us thy infant, hear our prayers through thine.

Virgin all excelling, mildest of the mild,

freed from guilt preserve us pure and undefiled.

Keep our life all spotless, make our way secure,

till we find in Jesus, joy forevermore.

From the highest heavens to the Almighty Three,

Father, Son and Spirit, one same glory be. Amen.

Litany of the Holy Name of Jesus

Lord, *have mercy on us.* Christ, *have mercy on us.* Lord, *have mercy on us.*

Jesus, *hear us.* Jesus, *graciously hear us.*

God the Father of heaven, *have mercy on us.*

God the Son, Redeemer of the world, *have mercy on us.*

God the Holy Spirit, *have mercy on us.*

Holy Trinity, one God, *have mercy on us.*

(Response after **each** invocation is *Have mercy on us.*)

Jesus, Son of the living God.

Jesus, splendor of the Father.

Jesus, brightness of eternal light.

Jesus, King of glory.

Jesus, sun of justice.

Jesus, Son of the Virgin Mary.

Jesus, most amiable.

Jesus, most admirable.

Jesus, the mighty God.

Jesus, Father of the world to come.

Jesus, angel of the great counsel.

Jesus, most powerful.

Jesus, most patient.

Jesus, most obedient.

Jesus, meek and humble of heart.

Jesus, lover of chastity.

Jesus, our lover.

Jesus, God of peace.

Jesus, Author of life.

Jesus, Model of virtues.

Jesus, zealous for souls.

Jesus, our God.

Jesus, our refuge.

Jesus, father of the poor.

Jesus, treasure of the faithful.

Jesus, good Shepherd.

Jesus, true light.

Jesus, eternal wisdom.

Jesus, infinite goodness.

Jesus, our way and our life.

Jesus, joy of the Angels.

Jesus, King of the Patriarchs.

Jesus, Master of the Apostles.

Jesus, teacher of Evangelists.

Jesus, strength of Martyrs.

Jesus, light of Confessors.

Jesus, purity of Virgins.

Jesus, crown of all Saints.

. . . .

Be merciful, *spare us, O Jesus.*

Be merciful, *graciously hear us, O Jesus.*

. . . .

(Response after **each** invocation is *Deliver us, O Jesus.*)

From all evil.

From all sin.

From Thy wrath.

From the snares of the devil.

From the spirit of fornication.

From everlasting death.

From the neglect of Thine

inspirations.

Through the mystery of Thy

holy Incarnation.

Through Thy Nativity.

Through Thy Infancy.

Through Thy most divine Life.

Through Thy labors.

Through Thine agony and

passion.

Through Thy cross and

dereliction.

Through Thy sufferings.

Through Thy death and burial.

Through Thy Resurrection.

Through Thine Ascension.

Through Thine institution

of the most Holy Eucharist.

Through Thy joys.

Through Thy glory.

. . . .

Lamb of God, who takest away the sins of the world,

spare us, O Jesus.

Lamb of God, who takest away the sins of the world,

graciously hear us, O Jesus.

Lamb of God, who takest away the sins of the world,

have mercy on us, O Jesus.

Jesus, *hear us.* Jesus, *graciously hear us.*

Let us pray.

O Lord Jesus Christ. Who hast said: ask and ye shall receive, seek and ye shall find; knock and it shall be opened unto you; grant, we beseech Thee, to us who ask the gift of Thy divine love, that we may ever love Thee with all our hearts, and in all our words and actions, and never cease praising Thee. Give us O Lord, a perpetual love of Thy holy name; for Thou never failest to govern those whom Thou dost solidly establish in Thy love. Who livest and reignest world without end. Amen.

St. Louis Marie de Montfort's Prayer to Jesus

O most loving Jesus, deign to let me pour forth my gratitude before Thee, for the grace Thou hast bestowed upon me in giving me Thy holy Mother through the devotion of holy slavery, that she may be my advocate in the presence of Thy majesty and my support in my extreme misery. Alas, O Lord! I am so wretched that without this dear Mother I should be certainly lost. Yes, Mary is necessary for me at Thy side and everywhere: that she may appease Thy just wrath, because I have so often offended Thee; that she may save me from the eternal punishment of Thy justice, which I deserve; that she may contemplate Thee, speak to Thee, pray to Thee, approach Thee and please Thee; that she may help me to save my soul and the souls of others; in short, Mary is necessary for me that I may always do Thy holy will and seek Thy greater glory in all things. Ah, would that I could proclaim throughout the whole world the mercy that Thou hast shown to me! Would that everyone might know I should be already damned, were it not for Mary! Mary is in me. Oh, what a treasure! Oh, what a consolation! And shall I not be entirely hers? Oh, what ingratitude! My dear Savior, send me death rather than such a calamity, for I would rather die than live without belonging entirely to Mary.

With St. John the Evangelist at the foot of the cross, I have taken her a thousand times for my own and as many times have given myself to her; but if I have not yet done it as Thou, dear Jesus, dost wish, I now renew this offering as Thou desire me to renew it. And if Thou seest in my soul or my body anything that does not belong to this august princess, I pray Thee to take it and cast it far from me, for whatever in me does not belong to Mary is unworthy of Thee.

O Holy Spirit, grant me all these graces. Plant in my soul the Tree of true Life, which is Mary; cultivate it and tend it so that it may grow and blossom and bring forth the fruit of life in abundance. O Holy Spirit, give me great devotion to Mary, Thy faithful spouse; give me great confidence in her maternal heart and an abiding refuge in her mercy, so that by her Thou mayest truly form in me Jesus Christ, great and mighty, unto the fullness of His perfect age. Amen.

Marian Examination of Conscience

A Marian examination is very fitting for all of Mary's "little ones," whether you are a child or an adult. Looking to our heavenly Mother as the perfect example of Christian Virtue can help us immeasurably on our own path to holiness. At an appointed time each day, take the time to ask yourself if you have practiced the following:

- Profound Humility
- Continuous Prayer
- Living Faith
- Universal Mortification
- Blind Obedience (Unswerving Allegiance to Jesus and His Church)

- Divine Purity
- Ardent Charity
- Heroic Patience
- Angelic Sweetness
- Divine Wisdom
- Seraphic Poverty

- Perfect Joy
- Resplendent Modesty
- Beautiful Honesty
- Radiant Tranquility
- Invincible Hope
- Tender Piety

Did we think of Our Lady today? Did we offer our work to Her?

Now, think of one thing you did which was not like Our Lady and think how She would have behaved in that situation.

Now, make an act of contrition.

Three Prayers of St. Ignatius Loyola

Take, O Lord, and receive my entire liberty, my memory, my understanding and my whole will. All that I am and all that I possess You have given me: I surrender it all to You to be disposed of according to Your will. Give me only Your love and Your grace; with these I will be rich enough, and will desire nothing more. Amen.

Grant, O Lord, that my heart may neither desire nor seek anything but what is necessary for the fulfillment of Thy holy will. May health or sickness, riches or poverty, honors or contempt, humiliations, leave my soul in that state of perfect detachment to which I desire to attain for Thy greater honor and Thy greater glory. Amen.

O my God, teach me to be generous: to serve you as you deserve to be served; to give without counting the cost; to fight without fear of being wounded; to work without seeking rest; and to spend myself without expecting any reward, but the knowledge that I am doing your holy will.

(This prayer is often attributed to St. Ignatius, sometimes to St. Francis Xavier.)

My Own Prayer

_____

_____

_____

_____

_____

_____

_____

_____

_____

_____

_____

_____

_____

_____

_____

_____

_____

_____

Act of Consecration to Jesus through Mary

O Eternal and incarnate Wisdom! O sweetest and most adorable Jesus! True God and true man, only Son of the Eternal Father, and of Mary, always virgin! I adore Thee profoundly in the bosom and splendors of Thy Father during eternity; and I adore Thee also in the virginal bosom of Mary, Thy most worthy Mother, in the time of Thine incarnation.

I give Thee thanks for Thou hast annihilated Thyself, taking the form of a slave in order to rescue me from the cruel slavery of the devil. I praise and glorify Thee for Thou hast been pleased to submit Thyself to Mary, Thy holy Mother, in all things, in order to make me Thy faithful slave through her. But, alas! Ungrateful and faithless as I have been, I have not kept the promises which I made so solemnly to Thee in my Baptism; I have not fulfilled my obligations; I do not deserve to be called Thy child, nor yet Thy slave; and as there is nothing in me which does not merit Thine anger and Thy repulse, I dare not come by myself before Thy most holy and august Majesty. It is on this account that I have recourse to the intercession of Thy most holy Mother, whom Thou hast given me for a mediatrix with Thee. It is through her that I hope to obtain of Thee contrition, the pardon of my sins, and the acquisition and preservation of Wisdom.

Hail, then, O immaculate Mary, living tabernacle of the Divinity, where the Eternal Wisdom willed to be hidden and to be adored by angels and by men! Hail, O Queen of heaven and earth, to whose empire everything is subject which is under God. Hail, O sure refuge of sinners, whose mercy fails no one. Hear the desires which I have of the Divine Wisdom; and for that end receive the vows and offerings which in my lowliness I present to thee.

    I, _____ , a faithless sinner, renew and ratify today in thy hands the vows of my Baptism; I renounce forever Satan, his pomps and works; and I give myself entirely to Jesus Christ, the Incarnate Wisdom, to carry my cross after Him all the days of my life, and to be more faithful to Him than I have ever been before. In the presence of all the heavenly court I choose thee this day for my Mother and Mistress. I deliver and consecrate to thee, as thy slave, my body and soul, my goods, both interior and exterior, and even the value of all my good actions, past, present and future; leaving to thee the entire and full right of disposing of me, and all that belongs to me, without exception, according to thy good pleasure, for the greater glory of God in time and in eternity.

    Receive, O benignant Virgin, this little offering of my slavery, in honor of, and in union with, that subjection which the Eternal Wisdom deigned to have to thy maternity; in homage to the power which both of you have over this poor sinner, and in thanksgiving for the privileges with which the Holy Trinity has favored thee. I declare that I wish henceforth, as thy true slave, to seek thy honor and to obey thee in all things.

    O admirable Mother, present me to thy dear Son as His eternal slave, so that as He has redeemed me by thee, by thee He may receive me! O Mother of mercy, grant me the grace to obtain the true Wisdom of God; and for that end receive me among those whom thou lovest and teachest, whom thou leadest, nourishest and protectest as thy children and thy slaves.

O faithful Virgin, make me in all things so perfect a disciple, imitator and slave of the Incarnate Wisdom, Jesus Christ thy Son, that I may attain, by thine intercession and by thine example, to the fullness of His age on earth and of His glory in heaven. Amen.

_____

Sign your name here   Date

Short Form of Consecration *(For daily recitation)*

I, _____ , a faithless sinner, renew and ratify today in thy hands the vows of my Baptism; I renounce forever Satan, his pomps and works; and I give myself entirely to Jesus Christ, the Incarnate Wisdom, to carry my cross after Him all the days of my life, and to be more faithful to Him than I have ever been before. In the presence of all the heavenly court I choose thee this day for my Mother and Mistress. I deliver and consecrate to thee, as thy slave, my body and soul, my goods, both interior and exterior, and even the value of all my good actions, past, present and future; leaving to thee the entire and full right of disposing of me, and all that belongs to me, without exception, according to thy good pleasure, for the greater glory of God in time and in eternity. Amen.

(For additional information regarding the 33-day consecration, please visit www.fisheaters.com/totalconsecrationmontfort.html)

Anima Christi

Soul of Christ, sanctify me. Body of Christ, save me.

Blood of Christ, inebriate me.

Water from the side of Christ, cleanse me.

Passion of Christ, strengthen me.

O good Jesus, hear me.

Within Thy wounds hide me.

Suffer me never to be separated from Thee.

From the malignant enemy defend me.

In the hour of my death call me and bid me come unto Thee,

That with Thy Saints I may praise Thee forever and ever.

Amen.

Prayer of St. John Vianney

"I love You, O my God, and my only desire is to love You until the last breath of my life. I love You, O my infinitely lovable God, and I would rather die loving You, than live without loving You. I love You, Lord and the only grace I ask is to love You eternally…. My God, if my tongue cannot say in every moment that I love You, I want my heart to repeat it to You as often as I draw breath."

Angelus

V. The Angel of the Lord declared unto Mary,

R. And she conceived of the Holy Spirit.

Hail Mary, Full of Grace, the Lord is with thee. Blessed art thou among women, and blessed is the fruit of thy womb, Jesus. Holy

Mary, Mother of God, pray for us sinners now, and at the hour of
death. Amen.

V. Behold the handmaid of the Lord.

R. Be it done unto me according to Thy word.

Hail Mary . . .

V. And the Word was made Flesh,

R. And dwelt among us.

Hail Mary . . .

V. Pray for us, O holy Mother of God

R. that we may be made worthy of the promises of Christ.

Let us pray:

Pour forth, we beseech Thee, O Lord, Thy grace into our hearts; that,
we to whom the Incarnation of Christ Thy Son, was made known by
the message of an angel, may by His Passion and Cross be brought to
the glory of His Resurrection. Through the same Christ, Our Lord.
Amen.

Spiritual Communion

My Jesus, I believe that You are present in the Most Holy Sacrament.
I love You above all things, and I desire to receive You into my soul.
Since I cannot at this moment receive You sacramentally, come at least
spiritually into my heart.
I embrace You as if You were already there and unite myself wholly
to You.
Never permit me to be separated from You. Amen.

Prayer Before Communion/Spiritual Communion

Lord, I wish to receive You

with the purity, humility and devotion

with which your Most Holy Mother received You;

and with the spirit and fervor of the Saints.

Amen.

Prayer to My Guardian Angel

Angel of God, my guardian dear,

To whom God's love commits me here,

Ever this day, be at my side,

To light and guard, to rule and guide.

Amen.

Prayer of St. Gertrude the Great

Our Lord showed St. Gertrude the Great that the following prayer would release a vast number of souls from Purgatory each time it is said.

Eternal Father, I offer Thee the most Precious Blood of Thy Divine Son, Jesus, in union with the Masses said throughout the world today, for all the Holy Souls in purgatory, for sinners everywhere, for sinners in the universal church, those in my own home and within my family. Amen.

~Approval of His Eminence the Cardinal Patriarch of Lisbon, April 2, 1936.

The Twelve Promises of the Sacred Heart

Imprimatur: E. Morrogh Bernard Vic. Gen., Westmonasterii, 1954

1. I will give them all the graces necessary for their state in life.

2. I will give peace in their troubles.

3. I will console them in all their troubles.

4. They shall find in My Heart an assured refuge during life and especially at the hour of death.

5. I will pour abundant blessings on all their undertakings.

6. Sinners shall find in My Heart the source and infinite ocean of mercy.

7. Tepid souls shall become fervent.

8. Fervent souls shall speedily rise to great perfection.

9. I will bless the homes in which the image of my Sacred Heart shall be exposed and honored.*

10. I will give to priests the power to touch the most hardened hearts.

11. Those who propagate this devotion shall have their name written in My Heart, and it shall never be effaced.

12. The all-powerful love of My Heart will grant to all those who shall receive Communion on the first Friday of nine consecutive months the grace of final repentance; they shall not die under My displeasure, nor without receiving their Sacraments; My Heart shall be their assured refuge at that last hour.*

* *We exhort everyone to home enthronement and to fulfill the request of Our Lord regarding the reception of Communion on nine consecutive first Fridays (remember to go to Confession).*

The Five First Saturdays Devotion

Requested by Our Lady of Fatima

"I promise to assist at the hour of death with the graces necessary for salvation all those who, in order to make reparation to me, on the First Saturday of five successive months:

1. Attend **Mass** for five consecutive first Saturdays

2. **Confession** (within eight days before or eight days after every first Saturday for the five months. Confession every two weeks will always cover you.)

3. Receive **Holy Communion**

4. Recite five decades of the **Rosary**

5. **Keep me company for 15 minutes** while meditating on the mysteries of the Rosary

6. Have the intention of **making reparation to Our Lady**"

(emphasis added).

Sacrament of Penance: Examination of Conscience

~Used with permission by Father John Trigilio

Provided Courtesy of: Eternal Word Television Network
5817 Old Leeds Road, Irondale, AL 35210, www.ewtn.com

In the Sacrament of Penance the Faithful who confess their sins to a Priest, are sorry for those sins and have a firm purpose of amendment, receive from God, through the absolution given by that Priest, forgiveness of sins they have committed after Baptism, and at the same time they are reconciled with the Church, which by sinning they wounded (Canon 959).

Act of Contrition:

O my God, I am heartily sorry for having offended Thee, and I detest all my sins because I dread the loss of heaven and fear the pains of hell, but most of all, because they offend Thee, my God, who art all good and worthy of all my love. I firmly intend with the help of Thy grace to confess my sins, to do penance and to amend my life. Amen.

Examination of Conscience

I. "I am the Lord, thy God, thou shalt not have strange gods before Me."

Have I sinned against Religion by seriously believing in New Age, Scientology, Astrology, Horoscopes, Fortune-telling, Superstition or engaging in the Occult? Did I endanger my Catholic Faith or cause scandal by associating with anti-Catholic groups & associations (e.g., the Freemasons)? Have fame, fortune, money, career, pleasure, etc., replaced God as my highest priority? Have I neglected my daily prayers?

II. "Thou shalt not take the name of the Lord thy God in vain."

Have I committed blasphemy by using the name of God and Jesus Christ to swear rather than to praise? Have I committed sacrilege by showing disrespect to holy objects (crucifix, rosary) or contempt for religious persons (bishop, priests, deacons, women religious) or for sacred places (in church). Have I committed sacrilege by going to Holy Communion in the state of mortal sin without first going to confession e.g., after missing Mass on Sunday or a Holy Day? Did I violate the one-hour fast before Communion? Did I break the laws of fast and abstinence during Lent? Did I neglect my Easter duty to receive Holy Communion at least once? Have I neglected to support the Church and the poor by sharing my time, talent and treasure?

III. Remember to keep holy the Sabbath day.

Did I miss Mass on any Sunday or Holy Day of Obligation? (Bad weather and being sick do not count.) Have I shown disrespect by leaving Mass early, not paying attention or not joining in the prayers? Did I do unnecessary work on Sunday which could have been done the day before? Have I been stingy in my support for the Church? Do I give of my time & talent?

IV. Honor thy Father and Mother.

Parents: Have I set a bad example for my children by casually missing Mass, neglecting prayer, or ignore my responsibility to provide a Catholic education by either sending my children to parochial school or to C.C.D. (Religious Education Program)? Do I show little or no interest in my children's faith and practice of it? Have I showed disrespect for those in authority, government or Church? Have I not expressed my moral values to them?

Children: Have I been disobedient and/or disrespectful to my parents or guardians? Did I neglect to help them with household chores? Have I caused them unnecessary worry and anxiety by my attitude, behavior, moods, etc.?

V. Thou shalt not kill.

Did I consent, recommend, advise, approve, support or have an abortion? Did I realize that there is an excommunication for anyone who procures an abortion? Did I actively or passively cooperate with an act of euthanasia whereby ordinary means were stopped or means taken to directly end the life of an elderly or sick person? Have I committed an act of violence or abuse (physical, sexual, emotional or verbal)? Have I endangered the lives of others by reckless driving or by driving under the influence of drugs or alcohol? Do I show contempt for my body by neglecting to take care of my own health? Have I been mean or unjust to anyone? Have I held a grudge or sought revenge against someone who wronged me? Do I point out others' faults and mistakes while ignoring my own? Do I complain more than I compliment? Am I ungrateful for what other people do for me? Do I tear people down rather than encourage them? Am I prejudiced against people because of their color, language or ethnic-religious background?

VI. Thou shalt not commit adultery and
IX. Thou shalt not covet thy neighbor's wife.

Did I have any sex before or outside of marriage? Do I view pornographic material (magazines, videos, internet, hotlines)? Have I gone to massage parlors or adult book stores? Did I commit the sins of masturbation and/or artificial contraception? Have I not avoided the occasions of sin (persons or places) which would tempt me to be unfaithful to my spouse or to my own chastity? Do I encourage and entertain impure thoughts and desires? Do I tell or listen to dirty jokes? Have I committed fornication or adultery?

VII. Thou shalt not steal and
X. Thou shalt not covet thy neighbor's goods.

Have I stolen any object, committed any shoplifting or cheated anyone of their money? Did I knowingly deceive someone in business or commit fraud? Have I shown disrespect or even contempt for other people's property? Have I done any acts of vandalism? Am I greedy or envious of another's goods? Do I let financial and material concerns or the desire for comfort override my duty to God, to Church, to my family or my own spiritual well-being?

VIII. Thou shalt not bear false witness against thy neighbor.

Have I told a lie in order to deceive someone? Have I told the truth with the purpose and intention of ruining someone's reputation (sin of detraction)? Have I told a lie or spread rumors which may ruin someone's reputation (sin of calumny or slander)? Did I commit perjury by falsely swearing an oath on the Bible? Am I a busybody or do I love to spread gossip and secrets about others? Do I love to hear bad news about my enemies?

Additional Prayers

Please see the following website for a wide variety of Catholic prayers:

www.ewtn.com/Devotionals/prayers/index.htm

. . . .

Hail Mary

Hail Mary, Full of Grace, the Lord is with thee. Blessed art thou among women, and blessed is the fruit of thy womb, Jesus. Holy Mary, Mother of God, pray for us sinners now, and at the hour of death. Amen.

Glory Be

Glory Be to the Father, and to the Son, and to the Holy Spirit, as it was in the beginning, is now and ever shall be, world without end. Amen.